"Love the direct actions t[
detailing HOW

Luke Barber, 2(

THE SPARK
TO YOUR
SUCCESS

Mindset Magic for Teens

TEEJAY DOWE

**The Spark to Your Success –
Mindset Magic for Teens**

First published in 2021 by

Panoma Press Ltd
48 St Vincent Drive, St Albans, Herts, AL1 5SJ, UK
info@panomapress.com
www.panomapress.com

Book layout by Neil Coe.

978-1-784529-46-8

The right of TeeJay Dowe to be identified as the author of this work has been asserted in accordance with sections 77 and 78 of the Copyright, Designs and Patents Act 1988.

A CIP catalogue record for this book is available from the British Library.

Testimonials

"I like how the book interweaves both text and exercises so that you can apply your understanding there and then. The anecdotes provide a personal touch to resonate with too.

"I think the best feature, though, was the quotes and affirmations at the end of every chapter because they both reinforced and further substantiated the chapter's message whilst providing a more concise quote that can be taken away by memory.

"I also like how the paragraphs are shorter and build up the message between them, rather than clumping it all together in one mega-paragraph. For me, it's then easier to follow.

"Overall, I thought the book was inspiring and I'm now looking at daylight alarm clocks!"

Evie Pearce

"This is an AMAZING book. Just by reading the first few pages you can tell how much effort and commitment has been put into this book (and it paid off). I also love how TeeJay's characteristics are put into the play and stories and advice that is given to help you love yourself and grow as a person."

Ellie-Rose

"Really like the piece on the magnification of behaviours and focusing on thoughts, acknowledging the connection between the body and the mind.

"'Learn something new' – and you DON'T need to be good at it!

"Leadership – acknowledging the traits in the people you meet in day-to-day life that you like and replicating them too!

"Love the direct actions to take and explicitly detailing HOW to change.

"The text nicely details a plan and builds up to giving strategies to deal with behaviours. It has a delightful tone and some great points. It really eased me into being open to the ideas later on in the text, the last half was fantastic in tying it all together.

"I also loved the way it branches out and talks in depth about perfectionism, reframing things like rules and traditionally viewed negatives, and acknowledged the aspects of toxic positivity that can occur. The text feels much more grounded for it."

Luke Barber

"I liked the stories and examples, especially the metaphor for life and taking a positive stance in the present as it changes your outlook in life."

Ellie Ward

Acknowledgements

There is a well-known phrase that says 'thoughts become things' and this, the second book in the *Spark to Your Success* series, is a testament to that. Before the first book was even written, this second book was already in existence in my thoughts. It was already a real thing that in my imagination I saw sitting on my bookshelf and on yours. Your mind and your imagination are the most wonderful, incredible and powerful gifts and I am excited to share with you some of the ways that you too can unlock the magic of your own mindset and turn your thoughts into things too.

I would like to take this opportunity to say a big thank you to the people who have been instrumental in turning my thoughts into this book that you are now reading. The magical Charlotte Foster for her patience and critical ear which ensures that the Spark to Your Success podcast is on the air every week and sounds fantastic. The marvel that is Anna Woolliscroft who conjures up the right words to put my thoughts on to the pages of blogs and books and all things written. The wizardry of Simon Chubb who is so brilliant at transforming the words into the illustrations that you will enjoy throughout the book. And to all of the parents who put their trust and faith in me to share my mindset with their young people in our conversations and coaching sessions which often inspire the content for the thoughts that become more things.

In my mind right now I am waving a magic wand and wishing that as you wander through the pages and chapters of this next journey with me you find the magic inside your own mind and create for yourself a more positive and empowered way of living.

Let's shine our lights into the world and be the Spark to Success!

Contents

Chapter 1:   Introduction   11

Chapter 2:   The state of our roads –
             a metaphor for life?   17

Chapter 3:   Take a positive stance in the present   25

Chapter 4:   A tale of two viruses   31

Chapter 5:   A second more deadly virus?   37

Chapter 6:   Learned hopelessness is a thing   45

Chapter 7:   All the good stuff lies ahead   55

Chapter 8:   Choose earplugs wisely   65

Chapter 9:   Choose earphones wisely   73

Chapter 10: Stay focused with discipline   79

Chapter 11: Dishing out discipline and consequences
             for breaking the rules   87

Chapter 12: Stop trying to be a perfectionist   95

Chapter 13: Are you being judgmental?   103

Chapter 14: Andrew's story about self-limiting
             beliefs and judgment   111

Chapter 15: Forgive and forget   119

Chapter 16: How to declutter your mind   127

Chapter 17: The power of focus — eliminate the
            stress of distractions   135

Chapter 18: Focus your thoughts to feel better   143

Chapter 19: Embrace your mind's creativity   149

Chapter 20: What can you learn from our
            great leaders?   157

Chapter 21: How to develop inspirational
            leadership energy   165

Chapter 22: Influencing behaviours for the better   173

Chapter 23: How do you make sure you stay in control? 181

Chapter 24: Goal setting — plot your future   189

Chapter 25: The circle of life   195

Chapter 26: Wake up happy tomorrow and spring
            into action   199

About the author   208

Chapter 1
Introduction

As I began writing this book, the second in the *Spark to Your Success* series, it was the middle of the Covid-19 pandemic. The world was in lockdown and things were beyond tough. Life was difficult for everyone, in many different ways.

I'm sure you are aware of this forced freeze in civilisation and if you're reading this book with no clue, hold this one thought: the human race is still here. We lost many loved ones to an almost invisible virus and life, as we had come to know it, would forever change. But we made it. Yes, life is different now but we still have life!

"The purpose of our lives is to be happy."

Dalai Lama

A once in a lifetime experience

Throughout this pandemic, populations across the world complied with a lockdown period that has been unprecedented by anything your or my generation (and the ones in between) have seen. Over 100 years has passed since the Spanish Flu, the last known life-threatening international contagion.

Many people endured an emotional rollercoaster with some experiencing deep negative effects from the pandemic. Equally, many people experienced positive outcomes as families and communities came closer and enjoyed a quieter life.

Times of struggle bring new hope

People took to looking introspectively (to look inside and question yourself) at their lives and realised that relationships and experiences were worth far more than materialistic objects and self-obsessed behaviours. People changed and made changes in their lives that, overall, were for the better.

You may have been through this reflection period yourself. Maybe you struggled or felt that you missed out on your final year at school, college or university. Maybe you couldn't work because your employer had to close. Or maybe you didn't have the ideal safe and supportive family home that is so important to young people growing up.

You may still be struggling now for any number of reasons – and that reason may be nothing to do with an international pandemic. It may simply be that you are finding it tough to get to grips with a specific area of your life. If this is the case, then this book is for you.

Even if you have read the predecessor to this book, *The Spark to Your Success - Helping Teens Build Resilience*, this book is still for you as it will build on the tools and techniques you have already gained. This book is about mindset and how to develop and maintain a positive and growth approach to your mindset.

A positive mindset is everything to holding your own

- Do you struggle to celebrate successes?

- Do you put yourself down when things don't go to plan?

- Do you compare yourself to others?

- Are you impressionable and feel bullied into doing things you don't want to do?

- Do you struggle to fit in?

- Do you lack confidence?

- Do you feel stress and anxiety and respond in anger, sadness or by withdrawing from others?

- Do you always think the worst will happen?

- Are you aware that you have bad behaviours when it comes to health, wealth, food, drink and relationships?

If you answer yes to any of the above questions, then you are not alone. This book is packed full of stories, methods and exercises to help you deal with, and overcome, negative thoughts and feelings and unhelpful behaviours.

My last book introduced the foundations as to why you think the way you do. It explained why people have different thoughts, feelings and reactions even though they experience exactly the same situation as you. It described what goes on in between your two ears and how your response to a situation stems from many factors.

This book is all about getting you back on to the track of a positive mindset.

The Spark to Your Success - Mindset Magic for Teens will equip you with emotional strength and give you confidence in your own abilities. It will provide certainty to stay firmly on the road of positivity and ensure your thoughts and behaviours remain true to your identity and values.

I will introduce you to powerful techniques that are grounded in scientific and psychological research, and you'll read real-life stories from those who have trudged troubled trails. You might relate to their struggles, but you'll also read with your own eyes how they turned their life around for the better. How they made a positive change. How they transformed their behaviour and let go of any darkness that held them back.

What you need to know is that *you are strong already* but you may have been shaken a little. It may be that you need to find yourself again. You may need to revisit past experiences and reframe the way you think about them or the future. Maybe you need guidance to find your true purpose in life. This book will support you to do just that.

You'll learn about transformation and what success looks like when you grab your destiny with both hands and never let go. You'll learn how to do this by tapping into the power of your mind.

"You only live once, but if you do it right, once is enough."

Mae West

Are you ready? Make sure you have access to the following:

- A pen or pencil
- A notebook or journal
- Some scrap paper or a post-it for scribbling notes
- A highlighter
- Access to your photographs and a camera

Let's dive right in and start a life journey – you're going to thank me for this in 25 chapters' time!

TeeJay

Xoxo

P.S. If at any stage throughout this book you feel as though you really need to speak to someone, I'll be here for you. You can reach me via my Back on Track Teens socials or by my email below. You can also share your thoughts and feelings with our growing community.

- www.instagram.com/ignition.rocks
- www.facebook.com/IgnitionYP
- teejay@backontrackteens.com

Chapter 2

The state of our roads - a metaphor for life?

Can you believe the state of our roads?

It's a bit of an odd subject to kick off a positive mindset coaching book I know, but bear with me, there is a serious point to this. And it's always good to begin with a story!

Pothole distraction and damage

Even if you haven't passed your driving test you will definitely have seen or felt the potholes (or to be politically correct 'surface defects') that are appearing everywhere in our roads. I travel a lot, locally and nationally, and our roads are shocking. I even bust a suspension spring on my car the other week from the jolt of a pothole. It's so annoying, I mean, it felt more like a crater than a pothole!

> "Distractions destroy action. If it's not moving you towards your purpose, leave it alone."
>
> **Jermaine Riley**

A potter's hole

Now I'm a girl from the Potteries, which is the affectionate term we locals from Stoke-on-Trent use to refer to our hometown. 'Why is that?', you might ask. Well, it's because Stoke-on-Trent (located in central England in the county of Staffordshire) has been the heart of the pottery manufacturing and glazing industry since the 17th century.

Anyway, enough of the history lesson. I was excited to learn not so long ago that one of the explanations for the origins of potholes was linked to my beloved Potteries and the Potters (those born and bred in the area).

Apparently, potholes are so-called because craftspeople used to dig up clay from the roads that was subsequently used to make the pots (bone china pottery).

Of course, this is a pretty old technique because it was back in the day when roads were more of a dirt cart track than a shiny tar road surface. In those days, people travelled by foot, horseback or in a horse- or mule-pulled cart and they knew the holes had been excavated by the pot makers. Insightful, right?

Anyway, back to modern day living and the state of our roads...

A roadwork rant

Something else I noticed recently is that roadworks are everywhere! When was the last time you were late for school or work, or got held up on the way to an event or class because of temporary traffic lights? It's frustrating isn't it? We have a roadwork epidemic!

I seem to get stuck behind temporary traffic lights on almost every journey I make these days and it got me thinking. You know what it's like when your mind starts to wander and random things pop into your head – like the state of our roads, the multitude of potholes and how irritating traffic lights are…

Delays caused by roadworks or jolts to your car when you hit a pothole are stressful. It's annoying for a couple of different reasons: (1) because you feel that time is slipping away and (2) because the situation is beyond your control. Or is it?

Yes, it's distressing to lose time or be late for a class or an activity. Yes, you can beat yourself up a little about what if you had given yourself more time to allow for setbacks or planned an alternative route just in case. You really shouldn't by the way. Just accept the situation for what it is and move on. Taking a bruise off your inner voice is not going to change the situation or catapult you forward in time.

Actually, potholes and roadworks are a metaphor for real life, so what can you learn from them?

"An obstacle is often a stepping stone."

William Prescott

Planning for obstacles

In the case of roadworks there is often a diversion in place. Have you seen these? The yellow oblong signs with black writing that are meant to be helpful, offering an alternative route to bypass the someone or something that has blocked your way.

That's all well and good, but have you noticed how these signs start off clearly visible and frequent, then dwindle to a tiny playing card size and disappear? Usually, there's a point where you start to question whether you're on the right path because you've not seen a sign for what feels like hours? Slight exaggeration there, but they do seem to become so infrequent that you feel completely lost.

The sat nav has probably been screaming at you to turn around because it's unaware of the diversion in place and to make matters worse, you're usually in the middle of nowhere and your phone has no signal. Plus, the desperation of a cool drink and a toilet break are making themselves felt.

At this point you start to feel anxious and uncertain about what to do for the best. Do you stop at the next shop or politely wave at a passer-by and stop to ask for directions? And to top it off, because we live in a modern developed world, no one carries a good old-fashioned map anymore!

"Obstacles are put in your way to see if what you want is really worth fighting for."

Anonymous

The traditional way to plan a journey

Before our technological revolution we had to rely on atlas books and town and city maps – ask your folks or grandparents if they have a *Reader's Digest* atlas or an *A-Z* local town map lying around. It'll be dusty but it'll be intriguing if you like to see how things have developed.

Routes would be planned in advance of you setting off on a journey. To be fair, it was a wonderful thing when the internet launched because a list of directions to follow could be printed off. Genius!

The point here is that people took their time to plan things in more detail. Nowadays, most of us are used to jumping in the car and speaking to the sat nav so we never feel the need to prepare anything in advance.

Is a diversion a metaphor for life?

This chapter isn't about me letting off steam about the state of our roads. Diversions, hold-ups and potholes are most definitely a metaphor for life.

Potholes are annoying because you often don't see them before it's too late. You might be aware of a road crater, but because you're busy and have so much on your mind, you just forget. One minute you're comfortably motoring on your merry way and the next, boom, a wheel almost gets swallowed up by a sinkhole and you feel somewhat shaken. Has that ever happened to you?

Think about this in your life. Did you expect to do well in a test and when the final results were released it was a real blow because they were lower than anticipated?

Maybe you spruced yourself up for a college ball or a job interview and your kid brother or sister spilt their red energy drink all over your crisp white shirt or baby pink dress.

Or maybe a super exciting activity was planned but you fell ill the day before and couldn't go. You often can't plan ahead for situations like this and it's easy for panic to set in as you frantically search for a way to make things better.

Temporary traffic signals are like our internal signals and imitate the point at which you need to make a choice. Life is full of roadblocks. People or things can stand in your way and prevent you from achieving something that you had originally hoped. This might be a loss in time or a missed opportunity.

An obstacle can also trigger negative emotions, thoughts and behaviour patterns. This is a place you want to avoid because it's very much like the one where you're lost in the middle of nowhere with a dry mouth, no map, sat nav or phone signal and desperate for the loo!

"In the middle of every difficulty lies opportunity."

Albert Einstein

Plan in advance but accept obstacles will always be

It's a useful lesson in life to plan for the unexpected. If you build up resilience and stay positive, setbacks will not affect you in a negative way. You will overcome troubles quicker without them leaving a lasting impact. Be passionate and determined about what you want in life and you will get there. Learn to accept that some things happen and are out of your control. Rise above them and move on – you'll be stronger for it.

Diversions are distractions and whilst they can be annoying, they can also be exciting and intriguing. Wait, 'what?', you might ask!

A distraction offers something new and unknown, bringing a level of anticipation. How many social media posts have stopped your scrolling finger, or TV adverts caught your eye because you just had to read or watch them to find out more?

What was it that caught your attention and made you curious? In the example of potholes and roadworks your alternative journey may lead somewhere that you never intended and that's exciting. You see, there are two sides to everything!

"Obstacles do not block the path,
they are the path."

Zen proverb

Always seek out the positive, be inquisitive and never let uncertainty overwhelm you. By doing this you will encourage your mind to look for the best outcome and get creative when it comes to problem solving.

Chapter 3

Take a positive stance in the present

POSITIVE

NEGATIVE

In the last chapter we looked at how roadblocks and potholes were a metaphor for life. I encouraged you to plan for setbacks and to see obstacles as something to be curious about rather than something negative that you have no control over.

"I think it is possible for ordinary people to choose to be extraordinary."

Elon Musk

You always have control over your thoughts

The more obstacles you overcome, the more confident you will become as you build resilience. The worst thing you can do is let the obstacles and challenges take control and pull you down with thoughts of 'I can't', 'I'm no good at this' or 'it's too hard'.

Yes, it might feel difficult and you might be uncertain about which way to turn next, but if you focus on achieving a positive outcome, it will be possible because what you think, you do.

At some point in life there may come a time (or times) where you question what you are doing, ask where you are in life and think about where you want to go. It may be that you wonder what life is all about, or what happened that made you choose this pathway.

Sometimes people feel as though they have lost their way

and are unclear about the future. If this happens to you, remember that you are not alone and that it's actually a good opportunity to renew focus through curiosity.

"If you find a path with no obstacles it probably doesn't lead anywhere."

Frank A. Clark

Flipping the negative

I want to illustrate the concept of seeing something negative in a positive light with an exercise that outlines how people can be described.

It's important to be conscious about your choice of words. Have you ever heard the phrase 'think before you speak'? It's so easy to react quickly in response to something or someone with an instant feeling without knowing the full story. Sometimes it helps to be curious about your feelings and to consider the words that represent how you feel before you make a decision.

Next is a list of ten words that tend to have a negative association. No doubt you will feel an emotion towards some of these words and you may have even used them to describe someone you know.

Take out your journal and make notes about what each word means to you and, if you can, write an example of where you have used it or heard someone use it before.

1. Weird

2. Stubborn

3. Picky

4. Anxious

5. Nosy

6. Timid

7. Pushy

8. Hyperactive

9. Aggressive

10. Nerd

The ten words generally have negative connotations, which means a negative emotion or feeling is triggered from hearing or seeing the word.

Next, you'll see another ten words that trigger a positive emotion or feeling. These words are very similar to the negative words, but could they be a more precise way of describing the person? They are certainly more accepting, warming and positive.

There's a card game available on my Ignition! website that will help you to feel magnificent every day. Each card presents a negative feeling or emotion, and underneath it suggests an alternative and positive way to feel instead. It's super simple and fun to help you build the habit of staying happy and upbeat in life – check out the link below.

www.ignition.rocks/product/ignition-change-your-feelings-card-game/

Finding the positive

Now let's look at how you could describe someone with similar characteristics to the first set of words but in a positive way. Each number corresponds with the number in the first list.

1. Unique
2. Determined
3. Detailed
4. Excited
5. Curious
6. Reserved
7. Driven
8. Energetic
9. Assertive
10. Intelligent

How much better do you think the person would feel being described in this way? Hundreds of times better that's for sure, and you would feel better too because you would see a positive reaction from them. Wouldn't it make life better if you did think a little before speaking? And that goes for your inner voice jabbering away about others and yourself too!

Never be a passenger in life. Take control of every situation, no matter how small your efforts may seem. Use positive language to describe people and situations and it will form the habit of seeing things differently.

"You have all the shine you ever need. Don't let people say you don't."

Donald Glover

Remember, when something appears difficult think of it as a challenge because challenges can be overcome when you take control and with positive mindset.

Chapter 4
A tale of two viruses

If you've read my blog or listened to the podcast series, then you'll know how much I like to share stories to illustrate important points and self-development techniques. This chapter tells a story that is 100% true and the learnings to be made are still very real and will always remain valid.

As I share the experience, I want you to imagine this happening to you and what you would do.

"Life is 10% what happens to us and 90% how we react to it."

Dennis P. Kimbro

Your dream holiday is on the horizon

OK, you may not be old enough to book a holiday on your own, but I bet you've still dreamed of a destination where you would love to visit, so go with me on this ☺

You have booked a long weekend away for quality time to relax, enjoy the sunshine and take in a spot of history. You've been excited about the prospect of this holiday for ages and can't wait to go exploring because you've spent many hours glued to the computer researching where to go and what to see on your trip and it's going to be a holiday of a lifetime. It's a solo trip, by choice, and you are psyched to have the most amazing time.

A strange infection invades a faraway land

Several weeks before your holiday is due, it hits the news headlines that a strange new illness has taken hold in a distant land. The flu-like illness has infected many people and unfortunately results in many untimely deaths, but it is confined to the other side of the world, so it won't upset any of your plans.

Life progresses as normal and a couple of weeks later reports start to surface that seem to indicate a second virus – one that is not a new disease, but more on that later…

As you make the final preparations for your trip, the flu-like virus is spreading to other lands. It's all over the news and the media is having a field day, reporting on its developments constantly. The news is very negative and people are getting worried – even though the virus is still far away.

The second virus is now more powerful than the original. It's spreading more quickly than the first and people all around you are behaving irrationally.

Will you still go on your dream holiday? Are you willing to travel despite the continual news about a flu-like virus and a second virus extending?

"Pessimism leads to weakness, optimism to power."

William James

Creeping closer to home

One week before you travel, several cases of the original virus have been identified in the northern part of the country you will be visiting – but it's miles away from your destination so there shouldn't be anything to worry about.

There are also a few infections of the virus in your country but none reported locally and you are young, healthy and your travel agent hasn't called to cancel your trip.

You notice that everybody seems to be talking about the flu-like virus and local supermarkets are being ravaged. People are frightened, panic-buying and stockpiling toilet rolls and pasta!

Hand sanitiser and face masks are virtually unobtainable because the advice to use them, alongside washing your hands for 20 seconds at every possible moment, is being distributed by the government and the media. Is this the second virus getting closer to home?

Friends and family are asking if you are still going on holiday and you are receiving some rather opinionated comments about what you should do. Are you still excited or are doubts starting to creep in and you feel anxious?

Too close to home?

Two days before you are due to travel, the first patient with the flu-like virus is admitted to your local hospital. The patient isn't a local resident but the hospital is local. People are scared and rumours are rife.

You are starting to notice businesses making money from the spread of the second virus by hiking prices and using shock tactics in their marketing – fuelling the fire of people's fear and anxiety. Many events are being cancelled, hugs and shaking hands are no longer allowed and established businesses are suffering.

Things are getting out of control and cases are growing in the country you are soon to fly to. Are you still packed and ready to go?

2:30am – an eerie hour

You are up and ready. By habit you check your email (who does that at 2:30am?) to discover that the flight you had booked to fly you *back* home has been cancelled. But you can still get there! What do you do? Do you carry on as normal and hope that you will be able to reschedule the flight at the airport or do you cancel everything?

If you cancel your flight there, and the hotel, there will be no compensation because you are the one cancelling and not the travel company. But if you go, will the helpdesk be open at the airport in the early hours of the morning? Will you be able to call the travel company and speak to someone? Has the second virus reached you and forced you to change your mind?

What do you do? Do you feel anxious?

To be continued...

Chapter 5

A second more deadly virus?

At the end of the last chapter I wanted to create a cliff-hanger a bit like the end of a Netflix series that you've become addicted to! Addiction is not a good behaviour by the way, but let's continue with the tale of two viruses.

The flight that was booked to bring you back home has been cancelled – what do you do?

You stay positive and travel to the airport.

Throwing you off course

At the airport departures entrance the environment doesn't look quite as you remember it and you follow the new one-way directional signs. All of a sudden you realise you've missed the check-in desk and have arrived at airport security.

You have had no chance to ask anyone about rearranging your flight home and at this point it will be difficult to turn back. Do you feel nervous? Do you have a rapid heart rate, headache, shallow breathing or has confusion set in? If it has, these are the symptoms of the second virus.

Within ten minutes you've passed through security and have passed through the duty-free area. You buy a hot drink to calm your mood and settle down to wait for your flight. You have no travelling companion to talk to and no one to run through what to do before you take action and there is only 40 minutes until you need to board.

You call the airline. A lovely lady on the other end of the line is more than willing to help and sorts out new flight details to get you home in no time. You're good to go. Wow, how easy was that? How do you feel now? Relieved? Excited again? Still a little nervous?

Embark on an amazing adventure

The flight is smooth and you arrive at the destination effortlessly and on time – you have avoided the second virus. Phew. Your taxi is waiting at the airport and although the chauffeur drives a little crazily (that's the norm here) you arrive safely, check into the hotel, unpack and set off to find a bistro for a tasty lunch.

You enjoy the most amazing adventures during your first two days. The destination is enchanting and unusually quiet for such an alluring region. Could that be because the people who didn't get infected by the first virus got infected by the second and stayed away? Anyway, you have the place to yourself, your own private viewing. Awesome.

"Always turn a negative situation into a positive situation."

Michael Jordan

Lockdown looms

On day three you have an excursion to visit the top of a volcano planned – it's the highlight of your trip. You are waiting for a bus near a local attraction (that you visited on the first day) and notice that the gates are still locked even though it's 10am and a small queue is lingering.

You see a man approach the group and, after a couple of minutes, they start to disperse, looking perplexed and shaking their heads. It turns out that the attraction is now closed for the foreseeable future because of the first virus, even though it's only in the north of the land. Seemingly, the second more powerful virus is taking effect in the entire country and the government has issued the closure of all attractions.

Your bus arrives and the driver announces there's no charge. Excellent, you silently think! You board with fellow tourists, thankful to be on an exciting adventure and being taken there for free. Just as the bus chugs off, a 'breaking news' notification vibrates your mobile. The country that you are in has just announced that it's putting 16 million people in lockdown to prevent the spread of the flu-like virus. Eek!

This will immediately increase the fallout of the second virus – do you know what I'm referring to yet?

You arrive at your destination and soon realise that the bus journey was free because the volcano you had so desperately been looking forward to climbing was now closed. You take a few photos and feel grateful that you were at least able to see the epic sight with your own eyes.

Disruption mayhem

Later that evening back at the hotel, you receive a text message from the travel company to say that your flight home has been cancelled. Does your stomach tighten? The country is in a state of lockdown and your flight has been cancelled. Will the second virus now take hold of you? Will you hand over your power? This could very easily be a turning point where fear and negative emotions take control. What would you do?

Here's what I did...

I had a brief conversation with my inner voice about whether I would get home. If I didn't manage to get home, what would the consequences be? And what would my back-up plan have to be if I had to stay? This was a point where I needed to reframe my fearful inner dialogue. I needed to take control of my thoughts, feelings and emotions and stay practical and positive.

From all my training and knowledge about the mind and behaviour, I knew that what you focus on usually becomes the outcome. So, I chose to focus on telling myself that I was not going to catch the flu-like virus *or* the second virus. I turned my thoughts to focus on the fact that I would get home as originally planned. There would be no other outcome in my mind. I was in control.

The slight wave of anxiety that tugged at me when I read the text had now disappeared because I was focused on my outcome. My mindset was positive and I was going to achieve my goal. I called the airline and another lovely lady rescheduled my flight. Actually, it was a far better flight, so everything was good. Phew, I'd escaped the clutches of the second virus yet again.

"Be not afraid of life. Believe that life is worth living, and your belief will help create the fact."

William James

A true story

The events described are true. This experience happened to me in March 2020, in Pompeii the ancient Italian city near Naples.

I had *the* most wonderful time exploring a city that was buried by volcanic ash 2,000 years ago and I would not have missed it for the world. Would you have done the same if you were in my shoes?

I consider myself to be a fit and healthy (and young in mind) person. I do not consider myself at risk or in a vulnerable group.

During the lead-up to, and throughout, my holiday of a lifetime, despite the obstacles that kept trying to derail me, I successfully resisted the second virus.

"Once you replace negative thoughts with positive ones, you'll start having positive results."

Willie Nelson

The virus of the mind

You may have guessed by now that the second virus I've been referring to is one that affects the mind. Its symptoms are fear, panic, anxiety and irrational actions. If not treated, the initial symptoms can worsen and develop into depression, phobias, bad habits and behaviours, and hopelessness will set in.

You choose your own thoughts and therefore you choose your feelings, your actions and your outcomes. When I was in Pompeii (and prior to my trip) I chose to protect myself against the second virus of negativity and scaremongering.

By no means do I want to pooh-pooh the devastation Covid-19 has caused across the globe (and will no doubt continue to do so as I write this book). It's been overwhelming, and the damage caused will be felt for many years to come. You will have your own opinion of the pandemic based on your experience, but once Covid-19 has been eradicated, is under control or a cure has been found, the second virus from the story will still remain very real. It affects people every single day and always has done.

What I did want to do by sharing my story was to be clear on how shattering a virus of the mind can be. This virus has been around since humans were first able to make conscious decisions and it will continue to plague us. The only cure to this is you and the decisions you make.

"Be the reason someone smiles. Be the reason someone feels loved and believes in the goodness in people."

Roy T. Bennett

The story illustrates how susceptible the mind can be, but it equally demonstrates how powerful the mind can be if it is used for positive effect.

Let me ask you this: if you feel panic, anxiety, anger, sadness or any other emotions that are not positive, how is this negativity serving you and the people around you? Is it serving you well? The answer should be no. If it isn't no, then you have let negativity attack your mind and hopelessness has taken up residence. The good news is that now you are aware of this you are in a place where you can change your mindset for the better.

I challenge you to make a concerted effort to find your energy, to obtain your fuel by spreading positivity and infecting people with helpful and upbeat thoughts and actions. Spread happiness, peace and joy to disempower negativity – it all starts in the mind.

Chapter 6

Learned hopelessness is a thing

It's your decision to take control and anyone who has achieved in life will say that you just need to take action. And the same goes for challenges and obstacles that are put in your way. They have happened so what's the best course of action to take?

First of all, you need to accept that you face a challenge. Once you've accepted it for what it is, you can get creative, adapt and re-route your way forward to overcome that challenge.

Even though there will be periods in your life where you feel 'hopeless', taking action is often all you need to get over this feeling of being overwhelmed. The strength that it brings will empower you to achieve even more and you will build resilience along the way.

Beware of learned hopelessness

Learned hopelessness is a thing. This state of being sets in when the action to change never takes place.

Hopelessness is where you feel that people, even the world is against you or has let you down. You feel that you are always unlucky, that things aren't fair and you can't do what is needed. But this is simply not true. What's happening here is that *you* are giving away *your* power and it's 'learned hopelessness'. The situation therefore becomes hopeless and you see no way out.

'Hopeless' is a negative word, but when you describe something as hopeless you actually put a lot more certainty around a situation than 'hoping' for something. It's almost as though the thing you are hoping for has been written off so what's the point in even trying?

What other outcomes are there?

Instead of writing something off, decide to be different and remove all other outcomes other than achievement. Be determined that your wishes will happen and remove hope from the equation. Hope alone won't make it happen because the odds are not in your favour and it can turn into hopelessness. Action is the pivotal point.

If, for whatever reason, something doesn't look achievable – and this will only be the case after you have put in the effort to take action and to try to accomplish your goal – then give yourself permission to move on.

Remember the exercise in chapter three where we saw the positive side to a negative? Well, at this point, see the hopelessness of a situation as a fresh opportunity to start something new, to set your sights on a new hope that is positive.

"Every accomplishment starts with a decision to try."

John F. Kennedy

Find hope at the end of the tunnel even when things seem hopeless

To illustrate a real-life example of hope being the lifesaver for a hopeless situation, I'd like to share Emma's story.

Emma is a fabulous young lady, who has been the subject of evil bullies at various stages of her life, but she took control and her hope and determination saw her through.

Struggling to fit in

I've been to a lot of schools. Every couple of years, I would move schools and so fitting in and finding long-term friends was something I had never really experienced.

When I turned 13, my parents decided to move to Ireland from Nottinghamshire. School started mid-way through September and by October 22nd, I had my first broken bone. It was completely unprovoked. I was in the cloister area of school and someone came up to me and broke my arm.

I had a thirst for knowledge and always loved learning even though it was a struggle because I'm dyslexic and dyspraxic. Being put on the spot in class was a challenge and I was excluded from certain lessons such as learning Irish. Teachers thought there was no point in me trying to learn so I was immediately singled out as being different.

Being singled out

Even though I made a few friends, some of whom had been diagnosed with learning difficulties, we were all seen as 'odd' by the majority. We supported each other in our own way but when I was separated from them when classes were organised by way of ability, I was alone and singled out once again.

It got to the point where my private locker was being tampered with, stuff had been defaced, even set alight, the physical violence hadn't stopped, and I used to get prank calls at 2:00am in the morning. Teachers waved it off as nothing, and even though the police got involved at one point, it only made things worse. I was getting quite depressed with it all.

I eventually changed schools but it wasn't long before I was singled out again and the bullying began. I was really struggling, wasn't engaged in learning and couldn't see a reason to sit my exams. I had pretty much hit rock bottom, had no self-worth or self-belief − I felt like I was stuck at the bottom of a dark well.

Then an opportunity arose for me to move back to the UK. It meant that I'd be leaving my parents behind, but my one focus was getting my GCSEs and going to college. I studied a lot at home, much of my knowledge was self-taught and at 15 years old, I came out with 8 GCSEs − 6 Bs and 2 Cs. It was hard but my 'why' was strong. I had this dream and it gave me an escape to something else I could do.

Moving on

I found college very different and a challenge. I was the only girl with 32 boys because I took a computing course. Computing is the one thing I'm good at, but at this point I still had no idea what I wanted to do with my life.

I got a lot of unwanted attention in college and it was difficult. The bullying wasn't as physical as in Ireland but it certainly wasn't easy. I'd fought so hard to get there and I started wondering if I'd done the wrong thing. I just got to the point where I didn't even really want to be at college anymore.

Then I took a personal development course and met TeeJay.

Rediscovering happiness and how to find hope

The course broke me – but it built me back up 10,000 times stronger. It made me talk about truths that I never really wanted to admit, but without admitting them I never would have moved on. For the first time in a very long time I made friends.

I still wasn't 100% sure that I wanted to do computing, but I knew A-levels and completing my education was the way forward. It gave me that extra strength to carry on and it gave me the extra motivation to ask for help. It really gave me that drive again. That was something I hadn't had in a long, long time and it gave me confidence.

I was this shy little thing that wouldn't come out of the corner and hated anything but the deepest dark, then I realised that there is more to life than this. I can stick my head out once in a while and say hello.

So, at the age of 17, I got my grades with 2 As and a C at A-level.

I realised that life wasn't perfect HD quality, but there is a world out there. What I wanted to achieve was achievable. I started to see 'me' for the first time in years. I realised that I was happy and bubbly and was someone who could make friends.

Emma achieved something amazing at such an early stage in her life and she did it by firmly standing on her own two feet, grasping her hopes and setting about making them a reality.

Emma didn't go to university after college straight away, for quite some time she worked for the charity that had given her a massive boost in life. She focused on a 'pay it forward' campaign where people were helped in some way for no reason other than others want to help. It's a passion for Emma and it was the first thing she felt strongly about in a long time.

Following another personal development event about a year later, Emma realised that growing up she had been listening to other people telling her what she couldn't do and had bought into the story that she could never do her dream job. She came home from that event with new inspiration and belief in herself and decided that not only could she have her dream career but that she was going to. That dream job was to become a paramedic.

Emma paid for herself to return to college and get the qualifications needed. She paid for additional tuition when she struggled with some of the lessons. She applied for university and got turned down at first but would not be stopped. She applied again, got in, completed her course and right now is a paramedic making a huge difference to people's lives.

It takes a lot of courage to acknowledge truly what you're thinking, how and why, and to pinpoint the light you need to reach up and pull yourself out of the darkness. Sometimes you can actually like being in the darkness because it feels safe. It's easier to stay there than to transform, be brave and move on.

It doesn't matter where you have come from because the past doesn't define your future. It's also OK to be different, a little quirky, a little odd – like wearing odd socks!

"Hope is being able to see that there is light despite all of the darkness."

Desmond Tutu

Is bullying an issue you've come across?

If you have been bullied, you might recognise Emma's story and the emotions of disconnection, loneliness and thinking that nobody will ever be on your side. But can you see how it is possible to find light at the end of the tunnel? Can you understand how to find hope and how to celebrate what makes you an individual?

Choosing to react and taking control of a situation with a determined mindset makes all the difference. Be a role model leader not a victim.

Chapter 7
All the good stuff lies ahead

In the last few chapters you've read stories about how determination and a change in approach (mindset) can enable you to turn a negative situation, thought, feeling or action into a positive one.

You have seen examples in the games and exercises suggested and real-life encounters that prove this.

When you develop resilience to challenges and obstacles, it is easier to focus on positive goals and turn your hopes and ambitions into reality. Even if they start off small, each little achievement will fuel your hopes and ambitions to become bigger, more exciting, more daring and more fulfilling. And the result? An incredible life!

It comes down to you finding and keeping the right frame of mind when you come up against an obstacle. So, where do you start if you're not yet feeling it or if an event or person has caused you to feel low? Hope is where you begin.

What does hope mean to you?

When was the last time you 'hoped' for something to happen? Whether it was hope about a place, a person or a thing… what happened that led you to hope for something to happen? Equally, when did you last *lose* hope?

Hope is one of those words that's super powerful in one situation yet a bit wishy-washy in another. It can be empowering and disempowering depending on how and where you use it. Think about the different versions of the word hope:

- Hopeful
- Hopefully
- Hopeless
- Hopelessness

Each variation of the original word has a different meaning and how you identify each variation can massively impact your thoughts, emotions and subsequent reactions. People suffering from depression can forget what hope means. It can lead to hopeful turning into hopelessness. It can result in all the excitement and anticipation dissolving into a numb and unmotivational state.

Hope is power

Hope can be a formidable force when you are at rock bottom. When you feel depressed and beaten your body lacks energy and your mind lacks clarity. This could be during exam studies, joining a new class or starting your first job. They are all challenging for different reasons. Hope could even be the determination emerging from a conflict with bullies at school, overdemanding parents or a clash of personalities with your teacher.

Whatever the reason for hope surfacing and being a guiding light, we've all been there. When you feel lost in a dark place and reach the point of enough is enough, the act of clinging on to hope is without a doubt the light at the end of the tunnel. It's the spark that ignites a change in your circumstances and the driving force to take action.

With hope you can become free from the pressures of exams because you know within yourself that you will achieve a great outcome.

With hope you can gain the courage to take an opportunity to learn new things, expand your knowledge and develop an exciting career path.

And that same hope can be the invisible kick that will kickstart your journey to earn money, experience new adventures or gain independence.

This hope is your positive mindset kicking in.

"It always seems impossible until it's done."

Nelson Mandela

Hope creates possibility

How does the sensation of hope make you feel inside when you realise that things are about to change for the better? On seeing the silver lining in a situation or the possibility of a way out, do you feel anticipation or excitement?

Being 'hopeful' gives you something to hang on to and believe in. In desperate situations this emotion can absolutely save lives and I've personally known some severely depressed people turn their entire life around with hope.

But in order for change to happen, this hope needs to emerge from your thoughts and feelings and take on a positive emotion of determination that leads to an action. A positive action. Because what you think, you do.

"Of this be sure: you do not find the happy life... you make it."

Thomas S. Monson

Combine hope with a clear intention

Hope combined with a clear intention for action is a recipe that leads to progress. Hopes should be your goals that turn ideas into something achievable. You will feel the anticipation and excitement involved in a journey that began with a small glimmer of hope. Think big ☺

When you hope for something but never act on that hope, it will never motivate you and you may actually start to resent the thing or outcome that you once hoped for if you view it as too hard to realise, too far way, too good for you.

You may even start to dislike the things that you perceive have prevented you from achieving what you hoped for and see them as obstacles you cannot overcome. These obstacles could be people, work or education.

Worse still, you might become fearful or anxious about a situation. This is when that dark place I mentioned earlier opens up and you slide further into a negative space and feel 'hopeless'.

Remember this: you give away your power when you hope without taking action. By initiating action, a desire and intent inside ignites that keeps you moving forward. With this sort of focus and mindset you will achieve more, achieve bigger and achieve it faster.

"Stop being afraid of what could go wrong. Focus on what could go right."

Anonymous

The power of hope

I want to demonstrate the power of hope to you with a little exercise.

Find a position that's as comfortable as possible (but not so comfortable that you might fall asleep) and close your eyes. Breathe in deeply and slowly and hold your breath for a few seconds before gently breathing out. Repeat these five times or until you feel completely relaxed and your head is clear of its inner chatter.

Imagine something you would love to have or to achieve in life right now. What would you choose to be different if that were possible? Push all other thoughts from your mind and passionately **hope** for that outcome to happen. Really **hope** that you get it.

- What are you seeing when you hope for this?

- What do you hear?

- What do you feel?

- What are you saying to yourself?

- Where is this hope in your body – what sensations do you feel?

- Does the feeling have a weight, a shape, a colour?

Consider your thoughts, feelings and any emotions that arise from those feelings for a few moments and think about the why.

Slowly open your eyes and if you feel ready to do so, make a few notes in your journal to reflect on later. Now shake off those feelings, clear your mind again and prepare for round two.

Close your eyes and relax. Adjust your position if you need to and take in some more slow deep breaths. This time I want you to know with absolute certainty in your mind that you already have this thing in your life and have achieved the outcome you hoped for. It's happening, it's yours, it's real. Notice the differences in how you feel, even if they are subtle.

- How do you feel?

- What do you see or hear?

- What do you say to yourself now?

- Does it have an identity, a vibration, a sensation?

- Has the environment or situation changed since round one?

Spend some time being present in what you are visualising, seeing and hearing in your mind's eye. Now open your eyes for real and capture your thoughts, feelings and emotions again in your journal. It's best to do this in the moment while you are relaxed.

Out of the two exercises, which thoughts, feelings and emotions did you prefer? Those linked to hope or certainty?

I've done this exercise multiple times and certainty always come up trumps, but the only way to be certain that certainty will happen is to take action.

> *"Hope lies in dreams, in imagination, and in the courage of those who dare to make dreams into reality."*
>
> **Jonas Salk**

Hopefully should raise alarm bells

Never be that person who says they will hopefully do something. Why? Well, what this statement is really saying is 'maybe I will, maybe I won't!'

There is zero commitment where 'hopefully' is concerned. The word hopefully is actually an excuse, a get-out clause in advance in case the task doesn't get done. The act of using this word weakens the entire context around it. If you can, ditch it from your vocabulary!

If you say you will do something, commit to it. Give it a deadline to make it more real and take action. It will take practice because nothing happens overnight. See each new day as a new chance to practise. A new opportunity to gain new skills.

"Life's under no obligation to give us what we expect."

Margaret Mitchell

I'm going to end this chapter by saying ironically 'I hope you'll now think about using the word hope differently'. And to clarify *my* use of the word hope is because ultimately the control lies with you.

Chapter 8
Choose earplugs wisely

When you listen to external sources – be that media news reports, social media content, podcasts, books, your own social circle or family – how your mind interprets this information will determine the subsequent feelings and emotions, and the actions you take.

A lot of this process (and the science behind it) is covered in *The Spark to Your Success - Helping Teens Build Resilience.*

Check in on BOB

To summarise what goes on during this process look up BOB, who visually helps to explain that your internal representation of external incidents is based on your experience to date (of people, places and situations) and your thoughts about the future.

www.backontrackteens.com/wp-content/uploads/2020/06/Back-on-track-teens-BOB-2.pdf

This internal representation of thought will determine the feelings, emotions and action (or reaction) that follows.

The key takeaway here is that in order to keep your mindset positive, take care with what you take in and what you block out.

What do I mean by this? If you focus your efforts on seeing the positive in everything around you, you can become an expert at filtering negative stuff or at least choosing how you react to it. The analogy of choosing earplugs and earphones wisely illustrates this perfectly, so let me add a little more perspective by talking about the real world. I'll start with earplugs.

"Few things in the world are more powerful than a positive push. A smile.

A world of optimism and hope. A 'you can do it' when things are tough."

Richard M. DeVos

Where did you last go on holiday?

Can you think of the last trip you took with family, friends, or even a business trip if you're a young adult, that involved travelling on a plane? Or maybe when you stayed in a swanky hotel or were fortunate enough to attend an F1 grand prix or similar high-profile sporting event?

Quite often, especially on long-distance plane journeys, you get to pick up a freebie toiletry pack that includes an eye mask, headphones and maybe a pair of socks or a blanket. In a hotel you might benefit from a combined parcel containing a shower cap, shampoo, soap, or a toothbrush with the cutest tube of toothpaste!

It's such a novelty factor isn't it? Even if you don't actually need or want the stuff you take them anyway because it's free. Yay – who doesn't want free stuff, right?

"The best things in life are free."

Luther Vandross

Earplugs – your barrier to silence

One freebie that I love to acquire is earplugs. You know the small squishy foam ones that come in pairs and all sorts of colours – blue, green, yellow, orange, red... I've yet to bag a purple pair so I'm keeping my eyes open!

It's funny because I don't personally wear earplugs unless I'm on a plane, so I'm unsure as to whether they work in normal day-to-day life. If I'm honest, I worry a little that if they do work then I might miss something important like hearing my morning wake-up alarm!

Do you wear earplugs?

I have friends that use them frequently. One friend wears them at night because she has noisy neighbours and another friend's partner snores loudly. They both use earplugs to block out the unwanted sound in an attempt to have a good night's sleep.

Hotels located next to a railway line or by a flight path often hand out complimentary earplugs to guests to help ensure they have a good night's kip during their stay – it's good for reviews on Google, right?

It's not just external loud noise that needs blocking out

Earplugs got me thinking on a deeper level about the whole noise concept. The spongy plugs are designed to block out external noise and make it quieter, but sometimes we need to block out a different kind of noise. The noise of external negativity, such as bad news, people moaning and groaning, useless gossip or hearing of unhelpful behaviours from people around you. This noise isn't from heavy traffic or a loud snorer, it's the kind of noise that you don't want to get sucked into listening to; it will damage a whole lot more than your eardrums, it will damage your mindset if you pay attention to it!

Can you think about a time when your friends or family were talking about a bad situation? Maybe there was a negative news story on the television or a social media post that made you feel a bit sick or uneasy? This sort of unhelpful noise is everywhere and it takes a conscious decision to stay away from its evil grip.

Avoid negative mood hoovers

Personally, I avoid negative people, unhelpful music, films and TV programmes, ruthless news headlines, and I even think I'm allergic to unenthusiastic people!

How much better would the world be if everything you came into contact with, everything you saw or heard, was positive? One hundred per cent better for sure because there would be nothing external to drag you down.

OK, I know this is not always possible and avoidance isn't necessarily the only option. If your parents are listening to the news or a negatively biased television show as an example and you can't turn it off or leave the room. Being able to manage negative influences and view them critically in this type of situation is the best way to take the information you feel is helpful. Simply disregard the rest and get on with your day. Again, it takes practice as with any form of habit change, but you will improve.

Your inner negative critic

Thinking even deeper about this concept, it's sometimes not even the outside noise or the negative people and situations that are the negative tormentors. It's even closer to home than you think.

Often, it's the noise inside your own head that needs to be blocked.

You have 60,000 thoughts whizzing around inside your head every single minute of the day – that's a lot of chatter. A lot of noise that is potentially negative, so it's important to be consciously aware of when your inner negative critic kicks in so that you can work towards quietening it.

How cool would it be if there were hi-tech earplugs available that could block out the chatter? Have you ever had those thoughts that seem to play on a loop inside your head? They go round and round, starting over and over again. It's like carrying a tune inside your head that you keep singing and can't get rid of – and it's normally a song you can't stand!

There's nothing good about the future

Your negative inner critic can start chattering away and put a negative spin on the future too. Thoughts can be negative in nature due to feelings of uncertainty and overwhelm, or the emotions of fear, anger or sadness attach to something that hasn't taken place because of something that happened in the past. When this happens and the thought relay loop starts, each time you think about the future it appears worse in your head.

You scold yourself about what could have been done, should have been done, or what you would do if it happened again. Yes, you might have reacted quicker or remembered something sooner, but can you change it now? Chances are that the answer is no, so don't beat yourself up about it. Accept what has happened is in the past and move on. See a future event, no matter how similar you may think it will be to the past, as a new opportunity and a way to do things differently.

"Don't be a victim of negative self-talk. Remember you are listening."

Bob Proctor

It's super important to block out the negative stuff and to hush the inner negative critic, but it's equally important to dish up the positive stuff in abundance. An effective way to do this is by using your earplugs wisely...

Chapter 9
Choose earphones wisely

When was the last time you wore a pair of earphones (or headphones) to listen to your favourite band or artist, a podcast, an audiobook or had an insightful conversation with a friend?

Music is wonderfully therapeutic because it motivates you to sing and dance and triggers memories from a time that the song is anchored to.

A humorous, creative and engaging conversation with a friend, a positive debate at school or a discussion with your family over dinner can be rewarding in its outcome too because you learn something new, feel connected to people and part of something meaningful.

Being creative and engaging our senses is inherently human and it's good to experiment with topics, styles and flavours. Everyone is different and it's good to be different.

Peace and quiet is beneficial – in moderation

Sometimes you need a little peace and alone time to recuperate your energy levels. This is great, you need some level of privacy to be in your own space and to avoid being interrupted by other people or disrupted by notifications, external noises or scenes. It's also more than OK to relax without purpose for the sake of enjoyment.

But there's also a fine line between taking time out to replenish and purposely blocking out the world and everything that's around you. This is how people start to feel social anxiety and depression because they become disconnected from people and the real world and start to turn inward for comfort. As you've read already, there's an inner negative critic waiting for you and this critic is ten times noisier when you only have yourself to engage with.

Connection is good for the soul

As a human being you need connection and social activity. Some people need a bigger dose than others, but you need it all the same. Spending time with other people, whether it is within an educational environment, at home with family, socialising with friends or at work, the interaction serves to top up your essential need for connection, for love and for companionship.

I will even go as far to say that it's hugely empowering to strike up a conversation with a stranger on a train, in the supermarket queue on in the park.

As children we were taught never to talk to strangers. It does make sense on one level because it's the human instinct of safety kicking in that protects us from the unknown. People of authority such as parents and teachers are in a position to protect us at that age, but as you grow older you realise that there is so much knowledge, humour, creativity and opportunity when you interact with others.

Fill your inner thoughts with positive stuff

I do want to throw a curve ball into the equation that may clash a bit with my suggestion to strike up a conversation with a stranger. That is that using your time alone, travelling on the train, bus, walking down the street or waiting for something to take place is a great time to fill your inner thoughts with the positive stuff.

What do I mean? Well, it might be seen as antisocial if you stick your earphones in to shut out the noise of the world if you are at home, sitting at the kitchen table with your parents or in a café with your friends, but if you are alone on a journey somewhere then it's an opportunity to retreat and be yourself with the noise you enjoy.

Think of it as an exciting activity to learn or reflect or repeat – something positive rather than an excuse to block people out. What you are doing is proactively selecting your preferred noise. You are making a personal choice with what you 'input' into your thoughts.

But are you making a good choice? Do you turn to doom and gloom if you're feeling down?

Talk to the hand, because the ears ain't listening

It never ceases to amaze me how many people watch a sad film or listen to miserable songs when they feel down. Why?

If you're already in a negative place, surely that's going to make you feel worse! If you had an argument with a friend or your homework grade was much lower than you anticipated, why would you want to feel gloomier? It's odd isn't it?

Whilst negative thoughts will appear, it's important that you acknowledge them but accept them and move on quickly. Instead of filling your thoughts with more darkness, sadness and anger through an emotive song or tragic film, think about what will work to counteract your low state of mind.

Could it be an upbeat playlist? A happy, funky rhythm. A song with inspiring lyrics. A tempo that makes you smile and encourages you to sing out loud.

The last thing you should do if you feel low is to call a friend who will relate to your bad thoughts. The best thing would be to reach out to someone who will make you laugh. Find joyful memories to relive and add some humour to your day.

"You are the choices that you make."

Brian Abbey

Choose your earplugs and earphones wisely

What goes into your head affects what you think. Consequently, what you think affects how you feel, and how you feel affects what action you take.

One of the best ways to put optimistic thoughts into your head is to fall asleep thinking about something good. Better still, pop your earphones on (or in) and drift off to sleep listening to an enchanting story, cheerful music, relaxing self-hypnosis or calming meditation.

Keep lovely thoughts alive as you fall soundly asleep and dream of all the amazing things you will achieve in life.

The powerful thing that will happen is that once your conscious mind falls asleep to recharge your batteries, your unconscious mind will stay awake and absorb the fantastic messages you are feeding it. And guess what? You will wake up the next morning feeling amazing and ready to take on the world. It's effortless and you gain great results.

If you're unsure, I have loads of playlists, podcasts, audiobooks and meditations that I'm happy to share with you. In fact, let's swap – connect with me on social media. You can find all the details in the first chapter of the book.

Be proactive about what you let in and what you block out. Listen intentionally, with purpose, and take conscious control of your earplugs and earphones. Let in as much positivity as you need and filter out the negatives. Acknowledge the negatives if you need to and be curious if there is something that needs to be worked on but don't let them fester. You'll be a better person for it.

Oh, one final point, be sure to use earphones or earbuds that are ergonomically designed for sleeping to avoid unnecessary pressure around your ear and the potential of getting entangled with the wire. You don't want to wake up literally wound up!

"A negative mind will never give you a positive life."

Anonymous

Chapter 10
Stay focused with discipline

How would you like to learn a proven technique that will support you to build a strong foundation in honesty and having a positive attitude? This is the stuff that creates champions.

What am I talking about? Discipline of course, what else?

What does discipline mean?

Discipline has two meanings:

1. The kind of discipline that is a punishment. You have been 'disciplined' for doing something wrong or behaving inappropriately, as an example.

2. The other kind of discipline is more about self-discipline. Having the commitment to your own standards and goals, to be consistent in the things that you do and feel every day.

Both meanings are equally important in life, but you often don't get shown how to be self-disciplined as you grow up, and therefore you don't see the benefits the skill brings. Even adults struggle sometimes, so I want to discuss how to bring the discipline duo into your life to gain structure and fulfilment.

"We do today what they won't, so tomorrow we can accomplish what they can't."

Dwayne 'The Rock' Johnson

You are in control of self-discipline

A new year, new term, new semester, the turn of a birthday, or maybe a new job are typical times to set new goals. Times of big change such as a home move, the start of a new relationship, a death or a birth can also signal a focus for goal setting.

Think about the last time you set a goal. What was it? When was it? Did you achieve it?

Many goals never get achieved. Goals such as a healthy diet, new exercise regime, less time gaming or staring at your phone can start off well but are often quickly forgotten. Why do you think people give up? Has this ever happened to you where you were uber ambitious at the start but the motivation just fizzled out somewhere along the way?

What goes wrong?

Put simply, goals are left uncompleted because your 'why' wasn't big enough when you started and therefore your motivation wasn't strong enough to keep you going. It happens.

Instead of following through with a goal you become one of the world's biggest storytellers – an excuse-maker!

When have you said:

- You're too tired
- Have no time

- Don't have the right resources

- Need more energy

- Haven't had the right weather

- It's too far

- The cost is too much?

And you know what? You listened to the voice inside your head (the negative inner critic, remember?) and it talked you into or out of doing something.

What's the solution to self-discipline?

First of all, you have to say that you are going to do it no matter what – with belief.

Secondly, you need to commit to a daily action, even if it's for a short space of time. Commit to yourself, by yourself, and for yourself.

Thirdly, it helps to have someone hold you accountable to achieving your goal. This person could be a mentor, teacher, friend, sibling or parent who becomes an external support structure. This is another reason why people give up. If you are not reminded of your 'why', and the bigger vision that you set out to achieve, your motivation can dwindle. A strong external structure will help to keep you going.

Parents and friends can sometimes be the worst people to hold you accountable because they sympathise and empathise and let you off the hook. This will never help, so make sure you find someone tough who will make you push harder and see your progress.

No one can be the best you other than *you*. The easy way out – listening to the excuses and not committing – does feel good in the moment but it will always feel bad later. Whatever it is will turn around and bite you in the ass. Guaranteed!

> "A disciplined mind leads to happiness, and an undisciplined mind leads to suffering."
>
> **Dalai Lama**

Stick to your discipline

Set your goals and get on with it without moaning. Just do it, as a well-known sports brand would say! Active participation in working towards the goal will always have a better outcome.

Being strict with yourself creates a future you that is truthful. If you are consistent, people will trust you. That future you will become someone who's reliable, which is a super standard to have. This future you is someone who takes responsibility and is totally respected by others. You will be inspiring because you are passionate and dedicated in whatever you choose to do. This is a quality that shines through and you will stand out from the crowd because you are persistent and resilient.

How good does that sound?

"You have power over your mind, not outside events. Realise this, and you will find strength."

Marcus Aurelius

Take the discipline exercise

Create discipline that will lead to self-discipline.

I'll admit it, self-discipline is boring. It's about doing the small stuff every day, every week and every month. It's the little things that add up to make a huge difference.

Whatever you want to do, you need to do it every day. Practise to become better and better and consistently do the basics regularly until it becomes natural, a habit and part of your routine. Think about how routinely you brush your teeth every morning and night. That habit had to start from somewhere didn't it?

If you give up, then you've let the 'pity party' take over. Never settle for less than you can be and never give up – you are already incredible and you can be truly magnificent.

Excuses become patterns in different areas of your life. It could be a lack of passion, drive, self-respect or simply not feeling worthy enough.

Nowadays there are a whole heap of struggles and mental health issues that develop as a result. Self-reliance through discipline shows that you can be independent from others, but giving in will never lead to success. It will have completely the opposite effect and create a path to feeling weak, helpless and directionless.

Repeating things and sticking to your goals might seem hard at first, but trust me when I say it actually creates a much easier life in the future because self-discipline in being consistent with the little things helps you to develop a strong sense of independence, resourcefulness and faith in your own ability.

Self-discipline will give you freedom and flexibility in who you are and how you show up to the world – you will look your best and feel your best. You become the best educated for yourself whether that is academic or skills-based, and if you take care of what you eat and drink and have enough sleep, your health, happiness and confidence will give you an abundance of rewards in energy and success. How you feel inside is a great measure of success.

For more inspiration around the topic of self-discipline see *Can't Hurt Me* by David Goggins, who changed his mindset to change his life. 'Cheer' on Netflix is a good example of discipline in a team, where you become part of the team, staying in it and becoming a winner, while Jocko Willink will leave you challenged in a good way.

www.davidgoggins.com/book/

www.netflix.com/gb/title/81039393

www.jockopodcast.com/

"Self-command is the main discipline."

Ralph Waldo Emerson

Stay disciplined and become a master at self-discipline to build a strong mindset.

Chapter 11

Dishing out discipline and consequences for breaking the rules

You now understand the importance of self-discipline, but what about actual discipline and the consequences dished out for breaking the rules?

'Noo!' I hear you cry! Rules are meant for breaking, TeeJay. We don't like rules. Rules are for wimps and people who don't know how to have a good time! I'm chuckling as I write this because as a youngster, as a teenager, or any age for that matter, there will always be sets of rules that you don't agree with… even so, you still should abide by them.

> *"Effective discipline is based on loving guidance."*
>
> **Peggy O'Mara**

Playing the rules of the game

Rules are made for a reason and that reason is for your best interests. Rules aren't purposely made to be annoying, boring, or to prevent you from doing something. Even if you feel this way about a set of rules, they were still created to guide and help you, to keep you safe and to set you on the right track.

Picture a 'keep out' or 'no trespassing' sign clinging to a high fence that marks the perimeter of an old derelict property. The place looks scary, possibly haunted (if you believe in that sort of thing) and you might be curious to take a peek on the other side of the fence. But those measures have been put in place for safety purposes.

The building might contain asbestos (a toxic substance contained within the structure of old building walls and ceilings) and be likely to crumble, or include dangerous materials, sharp pipework and basically anything that could cause serious injury. I know it's tempting to venture in – temptation has a strong lure to adults as well as teens – but it is an unsafe environment and the rules are in place to protect you from getting hurt.

Rules indicate what's right and what's wrong

Rules are created for a number of different reasons. They could be the laws of the land set to maintain order, respect and equality. To avoid discrimination, and to discipline bad behaviour as a way of reform. Rules help to protect people, the countryside and wildlife, help to preserve heritage, customs and history, and even enable inventions for the future.

Some laws ensure morality by creating boundaries for healthy, safe relationships between family and friends, education, employment, sport and social circumstances.

Without rules people would do anything without a care for anyone or anything and there would be chaos. It wouldn't even be organised chaos!

Consequences need to be appropriate, proportionate and painful

If rules are broken, there are consequences. And the consequences should be appropriate, proportionate and painful in order for you to learn from the mistakes made and to understand what the impact of breaking the rules means.

I'm not talking about a physically painful consequence, like a punch in the face or no food for two days. That would just be hurtful, vicious and completely unnecessary. I'm referring to consequences that are in place to deter the rule-breaker from repeating their actions and to guide them to making better choices should they face the same situation again.

- Learn a valuable lesson
- Modify behaviour
- Develop new positive behaviours
- Gain respect
- Understand responsibility

There are so many positives that can come from rules and consequences because you gain an appreciation for why different rules are needed in different circumstances. You will benefit from any support offered to become phenomenal in the future because you have learned from the experience. Plus you will understand the rules for the future – for when you need to implement rules yourself with your own children, or in your career.

The rules of the house are just as important as the rules of the land and morality. Do your chores and be kind to your siblings ☺ Oh and for the parents reading, please think of something more creative than taking your child's phone away or switching off the internet for every consequence!

Remember, dishing out discipline and consequences for breaking the rules needs to be appropriate, proportionate and painful in order for it to create change.

"Discipline is helping a child solve a problem. Punishment is making a child suffer for having a problem. To raise problem solvers, focus on solution not retribution."

L.R. Knost

What if your own rules were broken?

What would you do if a friend hurt you by spreading rumours or your partner cheated on you? It's important to think about your own rules and the standards and values by which you live. The boundaries you choose to create must be firm and followed. If not, then you will be seen as someone who makes hollow threats and doesn't carry through the consequences. In the eyes of the other person you have given them permission to be hurtful to you in some way by breaking your rules.

Remember this: if you get rewarded for bad behaviour by having no appropriate, proportionate or painful consequences, this then becomes conditioned in your thoughts and behaviour. In turn, this becomes a habit, which is a dangerous place to be in – for you and the person behaving inappropriately.

> "The best leaders are gentle. In our culture, we have been misled to believe that the tougher we are, the more respect we will gain, but that is simply not true. What we gain by being tough is fear, and fear is not respect. Respect is gained by giving it away."

Rebecca Eanes

What would be your discipline and consequences?

If someone you thought was a friend was saying bad and untruthful things behind your back, would you let them get away with it? If you choose to do nothing, you're actually saying 'it's OK to lie about me, please go ahead and lie some more!'

I'm not saying you need to physically reprimand this so-called friend, but they need to understand the impact of their deception. It may be that you end your friendship, report them to a teacher or stand up to them and correct them in front of the whole class. Your rules, your choice, but you remain the one in control and the one who maintains respect, integrity and value.

"Boundaries and discipline, when offered non-punitively and in the context of empathy and respect, are gifts we should feel proud of and one of the highest forms of love."

Janet Lansbury

View the rules in a positive light

Rules are in place for good reason. When you view them in a positive light for the benefits of health, safety, compassion, responsibility and all the other well-intended reasons they stand for, it will improve your entire behaviour towards rules and discipline – hey, you may never need to be disciplined again!

Have you ever been on the wrong side of breaking the rules? What did you learn from the consequences you had to endure? Everything that happens is meant to be a lesson in life and it's a choice as to how you act.

Avoid the consequences by being amazing and abide by the rules – it will help your mindset to become more positive.

Chapter 12

Stop trying to be a perfectionist

Have you ever strived so hard to do everything to the absolute best of your ability yet still beat yourself up over the outcome? The constant need to perform at such high standards is the cause of many teenage stresses today, but is it really necessary?

You might think that learning from the consequences of discipline and practising good self-discipline strives to perfection…

Are you trying to be a perfectionist?

Hello! As far humans are concerned, being perfect is not possible. If it was, there would be nothing to aim for, no big goals to set, no exciting adventures to experience and nothing to achieve in life. That would actually be quite scary and boring wouldn't it?

How many times have you heard friends or family members using the 'I am a perfectionist' phrase? Maybe you say it about yourself as a self-confessed perfectionist. There's no such thing by the way!

People beat themselves up, put themselves down and feel bad every day because they try to be perfect. They suffer from low self-esteem and feelings of not being good enough simply because they strive to be perfect. So, if this is you, it's time to stop being a perfectionist.

You are an individual

As a teenager you will feel the pressure to perform in exams, take on extra-curricular activities and live up to parental, sibling and teacher expectations. But if labelling yourself as a perfectionist is a source of stress, then make a change today.

Not being perfect is what makes you individual, unique and special. It's the very thing that makes you *YOU*. Stop beating yourself up about not being perfect and celebrate being human by embracing all of the things that make you *you*.

Sure, it's OK to struggle. We all struggle from time to time. What you find hard, someone else will find easy. But it's guaranteed that what someone else finds difficult will be a breeze for you. As you learn and adapt and get used to things being good enough, you'll start to feel less pain around not being perfect.

"People throw away what they could have by insisting on perfection, which they cannot have, and looking for it in places that they can't even find it."

Edith Schaeffer

What is perfect?

How do you define 'perfect'? I love to chew over a dictionary definition and here's what defines 'perfect' according to our scholars.

- Lacking nothing, essential to the whole, complete of its nature or kind

- Being without defect or blemish

- Completely correct or accurate, exact and precise

Hmmm… here's my take… if you're either spiritual or have religious beliefs, you might argue that perfect is possible, because in a human we are all perfect creations, but do you really think that part of you is missing, that you are lacking something inside? Well, you wouldn't be striving to attain perfection if you really believed that you were perfect already, so I still maintain that perfect is not possible at least in our minds and beliefs.

As for being without defect or blemish, argh! We have a mega industry born from encouraging us to improve the way we look. Some marketing tactics even make us feel inadequate in some way in order to sell the illusion of being *perfect*. How can you live up to perfectly airbrushed images in magazines, on Instagram and social media in general? You can't, and to be honest, if you were to see those people in real life, you already know they won't look like they do in print or on screen.

"The essence of being human is that one does not seek perfection."

George Orwell

Is the lesson not in the mistake?

Think about this for a moment. Do you not learn something when a mistake is made? Is there not an element of comedy when you recollect the story of a blunder?

In your future career you might want to be a brain surgeon or a lawyer and, if you do, I will hope that you'd be completely correct or accurate, exact and precise. That job will demand it, but in general terms you aim to be correct. The challenge arises when an error occurs because you have two choices: (1) do you blow it out of proportion and be fearful of doing wrong in the future or (2) admit that it's a learning curve?

We've all been there! Some of the greatest lessons come from doing something wrong, accepting shortfalls and sharing those lessons with others as you move on.

What does being a perfectionist mean?

I asked a few self-proclaimed perfectionists to answer this question and you know what? Every answer was different! So how can perfection be a thing?

Perfectionist A: "A perfectionist won't accept the fact that there are few things in life that are perfect, there are always little flaws and so they become obsessed with the flaws, focusing on the 3% negative instead of the 97% positive."

Perfectionist B: "A perfectionist is someone who's held hostage by the need to have something perfect before they move on. A kind of obsessive compulsive thing."

Perfectionist C: "A perfectionist is someone who keeps tweaking something until it's exactly right."

Perfectionist D: "Well I was about to comment that perfectionism is an unhealthy obsession and then I realised that I think I suffer from it in two particular ways, one of them English grammar – I think in grammatical sentences, so maybe it's a question of being perfectionistic with certain aspects of one's behaviour rather than being a perfectionist."

Perfectionist E: "I would describe it as having to create something real that is exactly as you see it in your mind, anything else and it's not perfect. Perfect is a nice word that conjures up the best that our imagination can create; if we believe something to be perfect then it is and so it shall be."

Perfectionist F: "A perfectionist is a strong, determined and highly focused person, who strives for excellence and gets disappointed when perfection is not met. I guess they're going to be disappointed a lot of the time."

You see, all so different.

Ditch perfectionism and remove your stresses

Aim for excellence in whatever you do because this is achievable if you put in the effort. It doesn't have to be perfect to be excellent and by thinking in this way you remove the pressure of impossibility and replace it with excitement.

Perfection versus excellence

Grab your journal, a paper and pen or your chosen app.

- Write down your definition of perfect. What does it mean to you?

- What are your beliefs about being perfect – e.g. if you're a detail person do you need to write everything down?

- What are your rules for being perfect – e.g. always take your time, be on time, be in control of everything?

- How does trying to be perfect make you feel – e.g. stressed, under pressure, are people waiting for you to do something wrong and judge you?

- If you were to replace the word perfect with excellent, how would that be different for you?

Once you have thought about these questions, run through points 1-4 again but replace perfect with excellent. Can you see the difference? What makes you feel better?

Perfection is just a deception of your ego

You have the ability to think, to act and to create. Ideas start in your imagination and become a reality by taking action – it's amazing!

You can communicate with others easily and effortlessly in the words you speak, the words you write, the pictures you draw, and even in your body language – you're an awesome communicator.

You have the most incredible ability to dream, so use your imagination and create other realities when you need to. You breathe without even thinking about it, you keep your heart beating without focusing on it and your body produces chemicals when it needs them at the highest quality in the right amount.

You have the ability to inspire others through your thoughts, your words and your actions, need I say any more? You don't need to be perfect to be unique, special, different and incredible in your own right, you're those things already.

"Perfectionism is self-abuse of the highest order."

Anne Wilson Schaef

Stay unique, stop trying to be a perfectionist and see your learnings as a way to embrace life – it will add to your gifted mindset.

Chapter 13

Are you being judgmental?

If you like things to be organised and have strong standards, there's a high chance that you are judgmental both of yourself and of the people around you.

It's easy to make snap judgments about things, situations and people, but it doesn't actually make them correct. How many times have you made an instant decision about an event or a person only to discover later that you were wrong and then felt bad about it? It's happened to me for sure.

When you judge yourself or others harshly or unfairly it damages the relationship you have with yourself, your own self-esteem, self-worth and the people who were judged.

"When someone judges you, it isn't actually about you. It's about them and their own insecurities, limitations, and needs."

Lulu

It's not good to judge

Write this sentence down to remember it and so you can revisit it often.

"The moment that you judge someone you lose the ability to influence them and appreciate their gifts and that includes when you judge yourself too."

With this sentence in mind, when you next catch yourself in the moment of judging, hold it for a second and change the judging thought to one of curiosity. Think, 'I wonder what would make such a great human do something like that or say something like that'.

Judgment can be implicit and learned too. Take racism, sexism and ableism for example. Nobody is born with a bias towards these descriptors or set behaviours around the issues. They are most definitely learned and usually by an external source imprinting an opinion that you may take on.

Rather than judging the heck out of someone and giving them a label, try to support them instead. Even if they do something that goes against your values and standards, or it annoys, offends or just plain irritates you, just stop for a moment and be curious. It's the easiest thing in the world to criticise but it will use more of your energy and it will start to pull you down too.

Have you ever had similar thoughts to the ones below following a situation?

- He didn't say good morning to me, he's so rude

- She didn't offer me a drink, she's so selfish

- He got home from work last night and just sat in front of the TV, he's so lazy

- She's always putting more lipstick on, she's so vain

- He's always fooling around, he's just so shallow, what a show-off

- She threw that whole pack away just because she didn't like it, she's so wasteful

… and on and on and on…

On the other hand, have *you* ever felt as though *you* were being judged? Maybe you said or did something at school and received a few disapproving or strange looks. Maybe you had a negative comment from someone about the behaviour they had witnessed (or thought they had).

Think carefully about these next points:

- Does it make you feel superior in some way when you judge someone?

- Does it allow you to feel better about yourself?

It doesn't feel good when you judge yourself so why should it feel good when you judge somebody else? In fact, it usually doesn't, so maybe the assumption made in the judgment isn't correct and perhaps there's a different reason for the behaviour you witnessed.

Instead, look for the positive intention of the person and the action.

"When you judge others, you do not define them, you define yourself."

Earl Nightingale

Don't judge a book by its cover

I know a wonderful young man called Andrew. I didn't think he was wonderful when I first met him (I probably judged him too quickly) and neither did anyone who attended the same youth course he enlisted in.

When I took the time to be curious about Andrew, I saw an amazing individual who had fallen into the trap of displaying unhelpful behaviours as coping mechanisms because of the judgments he'd been subjected to.

I'll share Andrew's story in the next chapter, but for now let me say that people are not their behaviours. A behaviour is an outward symptom of an unmet need, so when people display negative behaviours it's usually their way of coping with something they have difficulty with. Showing that person support – and not being judgmental – is the best solution to help them get rid of their negative behaviours.

When you replace the act of judging with curiosity you set people up to win.

"Most people who are criticising and judging haven't even tried what you failed at."

David Goggins

Turn your inner judge into a curious explorer

Is there someone in your life who doesn't always live up to your standards or values for some reason?

Grab your journal or a piece of paper and a pen or open a notes app on your phone or tablet.

- Jot down the name of the person (or people)

- Who are they and how did they fall short of the mark in your eyes that caused you to judge them?

- What labels did you give them? Annoying, lazy, stupid, thoughtless…

- What judgments and assumptions did you make about them before they even gave you a chance to show you who they really were?

- What else could have really been going on for them?

I judged a guy who I thought was driving recklessly on the motorway once as his driving appeared dangerous. Well, it was potentially dangerous, but I judged him for being reckless, inconsiderate and for being a low life. But what else could have been going on in this guy's life?

Maybe his wife had gone into labour and he was thinking 'oh my gosh I have to be at the hospital right now'. Maybe he had a call from someone who'd just had an accident and he needed to go and be with them as soon as possible.

You don't know what circumstances occurred to cause someone to react in a certain way and sometimes it's best to give people the benefit of the doubt. You don't have to understand or question the situation, but if you do, ask how you could support them by setting them up to win instead of labelling them.

As you move forward be kind instead of judging and see what a difference it makes to how people react around you and how the relationship with yourself, your family and friends improves.

"Be curious, not judgmental."

Walt Whitman

Being curious instead of judgmental will strengthen your positivity.

Chapter 14

Andrew's story about self-limiting beliefs and judgment

In the past two chapters we looked at perfectionism and being judgmental and how these two traits are indeed very negative. To demonstrate this, I'd like to share a little story with you about a young man named Andrew who was his own worst enemy due to self-limiting beliefs. Beliefs entrenched in low self-worth, self-esteem or simply negative thoughts about his abilities.

Meet Andrew

Andrew was a young man who attended a youth course I helped with. At the time he was aged 16 and had just left school. He'd been fortunate enough to find a manual labour job and although it wasn't a role that he enjoyed, it was a job that added a little money to his pocket and gave him some independence.

During the course, Andrew was the most disruptive delegate in the room. He was constantly seeking attention, talking loudly and inappropriately and he interrupted people. He wasn't listening to the speakers or to the other delegates because he was too busy thinking about how he could be in the spotlight.

He disrupted the course flow with untimely comments about going to the pub, how much he drank and how much he wanted an alcoholic drink. His diet was appalling and consisted of sugar, fizzy drinks and caffeine and, according to Andrew, beer! He was overweight, very unfit, had a poor complexion and was lethargic.

Andrew's behaviour was not only challenging for the speakers and course leaders, but it was annoying to the other students. So much so that by the afternoon of the first day they physically segregated themselves from him by moving their chairs, leaving a big gap with Andrew sitting there all by himself.

"Judging a person does not define who they are. It defines who you are."

Wayne Dyer

Does judgment help or hinder you?

Now, I'm pretty sure you've probably already made assumptions or judgments about Andrew. Perhaps you're thinking he's lacking in social skills or that he's rude or arrogant – and it would be easy to go down that route. Maybe you've decided that he's uneducated, only thinks about himself and that he likes to be the centre of attention. If you had been on that course with the other delegates, would you have got fed up with his behaviour and moved your seat too or maybe challenged him about it?

You'd be forgiven for asking him to be quiet, like many of the students did on the day, and to keep his comments to himself – not that he took any notice of those requests. You might even have considered asking him to leave as he was causing so much disruption. In your judgment you could easily have dismissed Andrew as a no-hoper as many did, and he absolutely knew it and felt those judgments.

In their dismissal of Andrew, everyone in the room, and other people like his parents, his teachers, his friends, even his boss and the people that worked with him, never got to see the incredible gifts and resources that Andrew had because his presenting behaviour blinded them, preventing them from seeing beyond the cover-up of all that attention seeking.

"The least amount of judging we can do, the better off we are."

Michael J. Fox

Looking beneath the disguise

I took the trouble to give Andrew the attention that he so desperately needed (and I do mean needed not just wanted) in a coaching session later that day. When there was just him and me, I could give him all the attention he craved and discovered that Andrew was an amazing soul.

Unfortunately, he'd been given some really disempowering beliefs about himself. He heard them so often from others that he'd actually turned them into his truth and thought they formed his identity.

His parents had split up when he was young and he lived with his mum and stepfather, who treated him with disdain and, unfortunately, were emotionally abusive to him. Andrew still saw his real dad, but after the marriage ended his dad become an alcoholic and was often in no fit state, or sober enough, to appreciate Andrew's company.

How self-limiting beliefs manifest

The emotional abuse and lack of attention from both sides of the family had taken its toll on Andrew, on his confidence and his self-esteem to the point where it was hard to find either in him. Not that they weren't there, they had just been massively reduced. Andrew truly believed there was nothing good about him and his lack of self-worth actually put him at risk because he truly didn't care what happened to him, whether he lived or died. Although he wasn't suicidal, he had no regard for his own safety either.

All Andrew wanted was to be accepted and loved. His drinking and talk of drinking were just his way of attempting to be noticed by his father and he thought it was a way to get noticed by people around him too. He just wanted to have something in common with his dad so he could hang out with him and feel that he was wanted.

"Don't concern yourself with the opinions of those who judge you. That is placing on them an importance they do not have."

Donna Lynn Hope

Love the person not the behaviour

People's behaviour is a noticeable symptom of a need that is being unmet. People are not their behaviours and that was so true for Andrew. He needed to be loved as a person and then his behaviour could change.

For Andrew, after receiving positive attention during the four-day course and some tough love in dealing with his limiting beliefs and behavioural patterns, he now lives his life and appears in a way to others that is very different.

A positive change

If you met Andrew today, you would see a confident, caring, responsible young man, who looks after his health and is much more proactive. He has a great big smile, is full of compliments and shows an eagerness to help – you may even get a big hug when he gets to know you! Andrew can tell you his strengths and his gifts if you take the time to ask and he is consistently taking steps towards the life goals that he's now set.

One of Andrew's dreams was to become a landscape gardener and after our youth course he enrolled at a local college to study the necessary skills. The college was 24 miles away from where Andrew lived so he travelled by bus each day. He was so committed to the course that one day when the bus was cancelled he got on his bike and cycled! He told me, "All I kept thinking was that TeeJay said if you want something badly enough you'll find a way – so I did!" Bless him, that's the spirit!

"The more a man judges, the less he loves."

Honoré de Balzac

Andrew is not alone

Andrew's story is wonderful, but it's sadly not a one-off. Many people suffer from self-limiting beliefs and find themselves on the receiving end of judgments that do not help. In fact, it makes a bad situation worse.

See the good in people and support them to fulfil an unmet need – sometimes a little positive attention and help to see what a negative impact certain behaviour is having is all that's needed to make a significant change. It will improve your mindset and theirs.

Chapter 15
Forgive and forget

Sometimes you might find discipline difficult because you feel as though something out of your control has wronged you. But here's the thing… something may not have gone your way, set you back, or prevented you from achieving something, but if you hold on to those thoughts it's another way for the negativity to start to fester.

The trick is to catch your thoughts and to work on flipping them so you can move on. One way to do this is to forgive and forget.

"True forgiveness is when you can say, 'Thank you for that experience'."

Oprah Winfrey

What would you change if you knew how long you had to live?

This is quite a raw question but it's also a valid one, so let me explain.

It was the activity of researching a trip to Pompeii that got me thinking about the importance of change and the notion to forgive and forget.

If you aren't aware of the history of the Italian city of Pompeii, please spend a few minutes reading about the catastrophe that took place. In a nutshell, the volcano Mount Vesuvius erupted in 79AD and the volcanic ash from the lava showered down on the people of Pompeii so quickly that life at that time was preserved forever. Everything about their time was captured in a moment and, as a visitor, you can still see how it was 2,000 years ago – now there's one for your bucket list!

The point here is that if the people of Pompeii knew their fate, do you think they would have made any changes? If you knew, would you choose to be happy or sad? Would you spend time alone or with those you love? Would you make amends in any way?

Stop wasting valuable time

Think about this. You have absolutely no idea how long you will be here for. With that in mind, do you want to spend your time doing meaningless stuff?

How much time is wasted feeling bad about the small stuff, comparing yourself to others even though you are unique so there's no comparison? How often do you beat yourself up over something that hasn't gone quite right but that is out of your control? And when was the last time you complained about being bored? Really? How can you possibly be bored when there's so much to do and see in your life?

What does that have to do with forgiving and forgetting?

So many people would live their life differently if they knew what would happen. Petty quarrels, anger, hurt, resentment, disappointment and bitterness towards someone or something that has happened.

In order to be free of these negative emotions, you have to be able to forgive. Life is for living and it's not worth spending time and energy on feeling down or annoyed, or even anxious and depressed.

Forgiveness is about being human. Living the best life you can by feeling happy inside every day comes from your emotions, beliefs and actions. I see many people in my line of work who are eaten up about someone or something, or an incident that's happened in the past. This experience has moved into their head and is taking up way too much space, causing toxic negative thoughts every day. These negative feelings are irritating and make people feel horrible inside.

If these negative feelings aren't let go of, they will show up as a 'dis-ease' (feeling uncomfortable or out of your depth in some way) and eventually a disease, such as aches and pains or worse. No amount of holding on to these feelings will change the experience because it's in the past. The people you believe hurt you will never feel your pain. The only person feeling the pain and hurting is you, so it makes no sense why you would do that to yourself.

"Weak people revenge, strong people forgive."

Anonymous

Forgive, learn and let go

Forgiveness is not about ignoring the actions of others. And it's not about forgetting either. Forgiveness doesn't make a situation or a person right or OK, but it does help you to accept that it has happened and that you can't change it.

You will need to remember what took place in order to change what it means to you, and to change the future outcome of anything that may happen again.

I have a belief that everything that happens to us can ultimately be used to help to shape our life positively. If something happened to you that wasn't great, the separation of time and looking back with hindsight or 'kind-sight' will help you to reflect on what took place and lead you in building a positive future.

When you have the chance to look back, eventually you will realise that you wouldn't have been able to do this or that, or met this person and had that opportunity in your life. If challenges didn't happen, you would never learn from them and you would never grow as a person.

No matter what happens in life, you don't need to forgive and forget, you just need to forgive and learn. Revenge will only feel good in the moment and it will always have negative consequences. While you are resenting others you are not loving yourself and that's only having a negative impact on you.

Take positive lessons from a situation of conflict and be the better person. Let it have an impact on you for the better. Let go of the bad stuff and reel in the good stuff.

Acting this way will also have a positive impact on those around you. It can make you wiser, more compassionate, a better son or daughter, a model student or team member of the month.

Time is precious and you will never get that time back or replace it.

Live life like you 'mean it' versus being 'mean' in it

Each day is a like a new blank page in a book and it's you in charge of the pen writing the story. Stop rewriting the past in future pages – it's like receiving the punishment of writing lines for being naughty at school. Did you ever have to do this?

Find the gift in the past and let go of the pains. Forgiveness is not about you forgiving another person for doing wrong. It's a myth. Forgiveness is about *you* and giving *you* a new start. Free yourself from the toxic energy of hate, bitterness and anger. Take that time and energy, and instead invest that valuable time into something that brings you joy, makes you smile, makes you feel better.

"I forgive people but that doesn't mean I accept their behaviour or trust them. I forgive them for me, so I can let go and move on with my life."

Anonymous

Forgiveness is not about being selfish or giving away your power, it's about being strong, selfless, and acting for you and your best interests by taking *back* your power.

Find the meaning of unconditional love and forgiveness and grow from it.

Chapter 16

How to declutter your mind

Now you're in the right frame of mind to make changes, learn from mistakes, form self-discipline habits and to forgive and forget, let's have a look around you.

Before you set any significant goals it might make sense to declutter a few areas of your life.

Declutter for clarity

Getting organised or planning to organise things, activities and processes helps immensely with all aspects of life. If you procrastinate (the cycle of never getting something done because you always think about improvements or put it off for one reason or another) then you might need gentle encouragement to sort out your tat! I say this light-heartedly because it can be a struggle to let things go, to say goodbye to objects, or to change a routine.

When did you last have a tussle to fit things into cupboards, squish stuff into drawers or push items under the bed? I know this battle very well because I have daughters and grandchildren! Stuff just gets everywhere!

"The first step in crafting the life you want is to get rid of everything you don't."

Joshua Becker

De-junk your mind

A declutter is a superb task for any time of the year. The act of decluttering does something to your mindset – it's a positive thought process. It provides clarity and focus because you need to ask questions about your stuff or the things you do in life. Ask yourself:

- What purpose does it bring?
- How happy does it make you feel?
- What memories does it offer?

Tidying up will make more space around you and this effect will transfer from the outside world into your internal world. It will free up more headspace to think more easily and declutter your mind, allowing more control over your life.

If this is a time for exams then a tidy up will help you to absorb your revision efforts more effectively. In essence, you are allowing your brain to retain what you are learning with more precision in its newfound space!

Simple things like a clear desk space and a fresh notepad will have a huge cleansing effect. Clutter is a distraction in the same way that a social media notification is.

"Enjoy the peace of nature and declutter your inner world."

Amit Ray

Are you an emotional clutter collector?

Dare I say it, but *out of sight, out of mind* is a regular situation in my office.

I accumulated tat and whenever I started to organise it, most of it could be binned.

Mess on my computer desk. Junk on the floor. Boxes on my sofa and piles of magazines on my table. Even my cupboards were fighting to stay shut against the paraphernalia lurking inside!

Sometimes you hold on to things for the 'just in case' moment that hardly ever happens. You've heard of FOMO (fear of missing out), well the art of accumulating excess stuff has to be just that.

Is this you? Do you hold on to things just in case? Are you an emotional clutter collector, who hangs on to items because of their emotional value and memories? It's great to hold on to happy memories, I can't argue with that, but some memories can be negative and that's when you can start to feel anxious, stressed or even depressed.

Sometimes we hold on to things because we can't face dealing with them at that time. It's important that you recognise if this happens because the same can be said for feelings and emotions. You can hold on to a throwaway comment made by someone who hurt your feelings on some level, the same way you might hold on to a broken pen because of where it came from. The hurtful comment has no place in your life because it's not true and is only the opinion of another. The same can be said for the pen because it has no use in your life other than taking up space.

"Happiness is the place between too little and too much."

Finnish proverb

Tackle the tat

Review everything and assign some kind of order so you can weigh up its worth. What has been hidden away that can be recycled such as plastic, old paper, clothes, shoes, books, stationery and games?

What can you reorganise and put away so that it is stored in a tidy manner? Maybe you need some new shelves or cupboard space. Could recycling an old shoebox work as new storage? They're stackable too!

Make it fun. Can you wrap boxes in paper or posters that mean something to you? If you're a bit of a perfectionist, try colour coding items and boxes with labels, handwritten tags, or stickers.

Make the daunting task of decluttering competitive! Give yourself an hour or 90 minutes and see how much you can get through. What about a race against a sibling or friend? If that sounds too competitive, offer support and de-junk together.

- Who can make the biggest impact? Take before and after pictures

- Who can fill the most donation bags?

- Who can sell the most and make the most money?

- Who can throw away the most, how many bags can you fill?

- Who can recycle the most – who's the most environmentally friendly?

"Clutter is nothing more than postponed decisions."

Anonymous

Tips to deal with decluttering your mind

It's easy to talk about tidying up your bedroom (and to do it) but decluttering your mind requires more mental effort. Follow these tips to focus your mind on a positive emotional clear-out.

- If you have an object, ask what memories it holds. If the memories are negative in any way, get rid of it

- If you feel the need to remember the object, take a photograph and write down what it means to you. Going through this process can often reveal that you don't have that much to say

- Some items might have sentimental value but no financial value, so capture the good emotions by writing down:

    o   Why you like it

    o   Why it makes you smile

    o   Who it reminds you of

You will find that organising and clearing out objects with emotional attachments will distance you from negative aspects and you'll feel lighter and happier.

Keep pictures and memories but consider donating items to charity or passing them on in some way. You will feel good from this act alone. There might be no room for sentimental items in your room, but there will always be room in your heart.

Once you've tackled the decluttering of objects, move on to your thoughts and memories. To untangle your mind, it's best to carry out a pen and paper exercise by writing down all of the unhelpful stuff that is cluttering your mind. Ask similar questions as you did with the objects:

- What purpose does it bring?
- Who does it remind you of?
- How does it make you feel?
- Why do you think this way?

Whilst you might find this process painful, it is simple and will help you to identify why you have thoughts and feelings. It will be easier to let them go and move on – have a good cry if you need to!

"The best way to find out what we really need is to get rid of what we don't."

Marie Kondo

Refrain from hoarding clutter in your external surroundings and your internal mind and create some space. You'll have a healthier mind for it.

Chapter 17

The power of focus — eliminate the stress of distractions

When was the last time you felt completely focused on what you were doing and nothing could interrupt you from the flow of concentration? What were you doing at the time? Where were you?

The power of focus is incredible when you truly experience it but how often does true focus happen? If you thought for a long time about the opening chapter question or you couldn't think of a time, then it probably doesn't happen that often for you. That's OK, we can work through it together.

Distractions are everywhere

When you are in complete focus you'll disappear into the task or activity. You will achieve a great outcome and have the satisfaction of completing something important or enjoyable. The challenge, particularly in our modern day, is not to get interrupted!

Would it surprise you to know that research suggests we get distracted every three minutes on average? There's a serious problem with this fact. When you get distracted it takes much longer to get back into what you were doing before, to get your train of thought back and your head back into the game.

Distractions make you less effective, less efficient, take up more energy and can even make something that is normally fun seem like a real chore because it drags on.

"Focus on growth rather than perfection."

Anonymous

Why is it so hard to focus?

If you don't set yourself to win or if you're not in the mood when you start a task, it can be a pointless exercise because you are fighting to be productive… against productivity.

See if you can relate to this typical scenario. For me this would be a project at work but for you it might be your homework.

You sit down at the computer or with your notebook ready to research or start a creative project and as soon as you're seated you realise you've forgotten to put something away or turn something off and you must do it. Distraction number 1.

Item returned to its home and you sit down to start again. A notification chimes on your phone from Instagram, Snapchat or a similar social network. You check it because it might be something important and we all know how FOMO is a killer diversion! Distraction number 2.

OK, message read. Back to it. But now you're thirsty and really fancy a drink. You'll be quick but it's essential that you grab one. Distraction number 3.

Ah that's better. You settle down again, feeling focused and sipping your drink. You glance at your phone and see an email or text message pop up. You have to read and reply, right? Distraction number 4.

Phew, now that's all sorted, time to knuckle down. Mind you, maybe you should nip to the loo because you don't want that sensation disturbing you later. Distraction number 5.

Great, now you're refreshed, in the mood and you manage to crack on for ten minutes. Your phone rings. Distraction number 6.

Phone call dealt with and you're back in focus for a further ten minutes, but a deep groan resonates in your belly and you feel peckish. Time for a snack? Distraction number 7.

You pop downstairs to make a snack and see a letter on the side that grabs your attention and you tear it open. Distraction number 8.

Nothing to worry about in the letter, it could have waited. Never mind, you're back at the desk and ready to work. Darn it, you forgot your snack because you read the letter! Distraction number 9.

And so, the process of distraction continues with notifications, phone calls, people, wandering thoughts, scenes from beyond the window.

Have you ever wanted to carry out research for a school project, find a song to play, read about a place to visit online? Before you know it you've lost yourself down a rabbit hole as headlines grab your attention, images catch your eye or sounds tug at your curiosity. It's nonstop unless you do something about it.

"Good habits formed at youth make all the difference."

Aristotle

Shut out distractions and get stuff done

Interruptions can cause unwanted stress and anxiety, especially if you feel as though you can't get anything done. You may even start to resent the things or people that cause the distraction.

Multitasking is suggested as being a good trait. But is it really when you barely concentrate on one or another task before you switch again? Ask yourself if you are really doing two things at one time, or are you doing a few seconds of one and a few seconds of another and so on? Be honest with yourself. Take control of the situation and get your focus back.

Sometimes you deliberately don't shut out distractions because you actually don't want to do the task ahead. This can be an unconscious action and when you are in this state of mind you will see every interruption as important and will want to deal with them immediately, even if they are trivial.

"Life is like a camera. Just focus on what's important and capture the good times, develop from the negatives and if things don't work out, just take another shot."

Anonymous

The power of focus exercise

This exercise will require some thought in advance and a spot of planning and preparation (although not too much for those who hate the thought of planning).

- Decide what task you want to do and when to do it – this can be homework, creative painting, learning how to play a new tune, practising sports or taking a walk outside – whatever you like

- Turn off all notifications – your smart watch, Fitbit or other device and disable all notifications

- Turn your phone off or put it out of sight so you can't see it if it's on silent

- Make a drink, grab a snack and go to the loo

- Gather your paper, a pen, pencil, notebook and place them next to you (or in your bag if you're going outside) to allow your thoughts to be captured for later

- And finally, if there are other people around ask them not to disturb you for a set period of time. Pop a note on your door, add an auto-response to emails and a do not disturb to your messages

By going through all of these steps you will set yourself up to win, I guarantee it.

"Focus on your strengths."

Gary Vaynerchuk

Stay undistracted and get stuff done – your mind will stay clear, you'll feel more productive and you'll complete tasks quicker.

Chapter 18

Focus your thoughts to feel better

In the last two chapters you looked at the multitude of distractions that plague you every day and how focus can be used to eliminate conscious and unconscious interruptions.

Sharpening your focus to zoom in on what matters is all about selecting positive things that serve you well. The things that bring you joy, opportunities and make you feel incredible.

Your experience of the world is created through your thoughts, and what you focus on is usually what you'll get. Where your focus lies is where your energy will flow although I must point out that this can be both a positive or a negative flow.

Behaviour magnifies when times are tough

You have around 60,000 thoughts every day and the pandemic of 2020 caused a great many people to focus on negative things. Was this you?

It's interesting because people's behaviours didn't change, they just magnified due to the stress, change and uncertainty. The worriers magnified their worrying, the stressers stressed more, the carers cared more and the naturally grateful people were even more grateful and active in looking for things to be grateful about. The angry got angrier and the happy people chose to be happier, even if it was to counterbalance the unhappy people!

No matter what happens in the outside world, there has to be balance for you. I want to encourage positive vibes by helping you to focus your thoughts on the things that serve you well and make you feel good in order for you to strive for greatness.

"The thing that lies at the foundation of positive change, the way I see it, is service to a fellow human being."

Lee Lacocca

What are you focusing on?

What you focus on is what you get and the more you get, the more you focus on it – it's a circular process. To illustrate this, I want to introduce a little 'noticing' exercise.

Grab a piece of paper and a pencil, pen, coloured felt tips, crayons or whatever you can lay your hands on.

Take a moment to think about:

- What thoughts you have had in the last couple of days?

- Where has your focus been?

- What thoughts were more noticeable than others?

- How often did you think about the same things?

Write a list of everything that's been on your mind and how long you spent thinking about them. As you do this, pay attention to how you are feeling *now* and note the emotions you are feeling around each item on your list. Do you feel happy, curious, sad, angry, irritated or uncertain? You should feel different about each item.

Let's take this a step further and have a play with some ideas and focus on new thoughts with one condition: you can only add the ideas if they make you feel good. Leave anything negative off the list. Are you ready?

- **Focus your thoughts – connect**

  Focus on one way that you can connect with a friend today. Make it a friend who you haven't seen for a long time or someone you need to make more of an effort with. How will you connect? Zoom, House Party, Facetime, WhatsApp or Messenger. Could you show an elderly relative or younger sibling how to use their phone or computer to see and hear their loved ones?

- **Focus your thoughts – learn something new**

  Focus on one new thing that you can learn today. Will it be to brush up your cooking skills, bake a cake, nail a piece of homework or learn a new exercise? Could you start to learn a new language, sign language, a dance routine, a musical instrument or a spot of DIY to help your folks around the house?

- **Focus your thoughts – find something fun**

  How about watching a hilarious comedy, reading an enthralling book, listening to upbeat tunes, writing music or lyrics to a song or a poem? Could you draw, sketch, paint or create something crafty?

It's that simple. Three easy ways to change your focus into something positive and joyful.

Now you have done this exercise once, make it a habit. Focus your thoughts on something positive and make it a real action every day for the next few weeks. It will soon become a natural way for you to focus and you'll also notice how it changes your mood and actions for the better.

How can you help others?

Focus is not just about you. Think about how you can help others. Help out with chores at home, tidy up, wash the dishes, clean the kitchen, vacuum or dust. It feels good to help out and it feels amazing for others too – plus they will really appreciate you for your efforts.

Have you ever thought about volunteering at the local charity shop, animal rescue centre, a conservation community or food kitchen? It's so rewarding, try it.

What are you grateful for?

One of the most powerful acts you can do is think about what you are grateful for. Write your answers every day in a blank journal or buy a printed gratitude book to record how you feel. Ask yourself:

- What am I grateful for today?
- What am I proud of today?

- What am I excited about today?

- What did I learn today?

- How did I achieve today?

Switch boredom to curiosity, irritation or anxiety to hope, and take action to make that hope turn into plans to get excited about. Be fun, be positive and look forward to something that you can celebrate as an amazing achievement.

The more you shift your focus towards what you want, the more you'll get what you want – that's the rules. So, if you're going to focus on something you might as well focus on the happy stuff, right?

"In every day, there are 1,440 minutes. That means we have 1,440 daily opportunities to make a positive impact."

Les Brown

As you change your frame of thinking and carry out these exercises you will become more resourceful, generate more ideas, feel happier and be in complete flow every single day! How great is that?

Chapter 19
Embrace your mind's creativity

How amazing is your mind?

In this chapter I want to draw attention to the amazing abilities of your mind. It is there to protect you and keep you safe, but it's also the source of incredible inspiration and determination if you listen to it in a curious and positive manner.

It's great to research things that capture your curiosity. If you don't understand something in a text or that you might have heard on the radio or spoken by a friend, look it up to enhance your knowledge. YouTube is great for visual learners and there is an abundance of good stuff waiting to be found on social media and news apps to ignite your imagination.

Your imagination creates fantasy worlds where you escape at will into another dimension, full of the most amazing adventures, ingenious inventions, courageous acts, daring deeds, divine romances, hilarious scenarios and interesting stories.

"If you believe you can, you probably can. If you believe you won't, you most assuredly won't. Belief is the ignition switch that gets you off the launching pad."

Denis Waitley

Where do you go?

When you escape from reality, what alternative existence do you seek? Is it a safe and calming space, an action-packed environment or a wondrous secret place? Your mind's eye conjures magic, superheroes and magnificent superpowers that create the seeds and thoughts that turn into the great storybooks, films and games that you might play out throughout life.

Using the power of your mind is how you learn and expand, and subsequently discover new things that inspire you to do things differently in the real world. Everything around you was created by a seed of thought in someone's mind. Every invention came from a miniscule idea that developed because someone believed in it.

With distractions out of the way, tap into your innermost creativity and truly connect with your imagination. Let me explain this with another story.

The story of buried treasure

There's an old tale called 'Buried Treasure' by Paulo Coelho from the Sufi traditions of his book *The Alchemist* that has a powerful moral.

You can find this story and many other tales with important life-lesson meanings in a book called *The Magic of Metaphor* by Nick Owen, which is for teachers, trainers and thinkers.

www.amazon.co.uk/Magic-Metaphor-teachers-trainers-thinkers/dp/1899836705

Let's see what you think…

Many years ago, in a remote part of Wales lived a young man. He was a shepherd and spent his days and nights looking after the few sheep he'd inherited from his parents. He was a poor man because the sheep brought him little income. He barely had enough to eat or warm clothes but he had his dreams. Vibrant dreams of a successful future where he saw himself studying and using his knowledge to make a great impression on the world.

He dreamed of a world where all young people had the opportunity to go to school and study in order to improve the quality of their lives and multiply their opportunities.

The shepherd loved the sheep in his care, the beauty of the countryside, the passing of the seasons and the joy of waking to each new day, but he sensed there was more to life. Somehow, he knew that to achieve what he wanted he would have to make his own fortune.

A dream of inspiration

In the summer months the shepherd would spend time in the high pastures of the quiet solitary Welsh hills. Often he would sleep in the ruins of an abandoned chapel, curled up beside the stone walls, sheltering under what remained of the roof and protected from the weather by the leaves of a giant oak tree that grew within.

One night as he slept, the young man had a dream that planted a seed. In his dream, a strange figure dressed in white and green robes came to him and said, "Why do you remain here if you wish to follow your dreams? Wake up and take action, do not wait for the world to give you what you seek. Go to London, find your fortune on London Bridge."

And so the acorn in the young man's mind began to grow.

The power of your mind

Soon after his dream revelation, the young man sold his herd and packing sheep's cheese to eat and pure Welsh spring water to drink, he crossed wide valleys and roaring rivers, skirted sprawling cities and peaked high hills heading south and east until finally he arrived at the great metropolis of London.

In those days London Bridge was very different from today. It had many arches with a multitude of shops and houses on its banks. The bridge was crowded, bristling with all kinds of life, merchants shouting from their doorways, horses and carts bringing people and animals to and from the market – an abundance of sights, smells and sounds of bustling city life.

The young shepherd was mesmerised, he had never seen so much activity, heard so much noise or felt so much excitement in his life, but he was on a mission to find his fortune. He walked along the length of the bridge to find his destiny and then he walked back to see where he might have missed it. He retraced his steps, backwards and forwards, and searched long into the night until he was exhausted and finally slumped in a shop doorway and slept, dreaming of his sheep that he now very much missed.

Finding his fortune

At 6am he was woken suddenly by a sharp kick in the ribs. "Oi get up!" roared the merchant whose doorway the shepherd had slept in. "I watched you yesterday walking up and down staring into shops, looking at cracks in the paving stones and watching people and carts. I've a good mind to turn you over to the law. What's your game, son?"

"I came here to look for my fortune," stammered the shepherd, "I had a dream."

As a small crowd gathered the merchant rolled his eyes. "You'll have to do better than that, sunshine. Tell us about the dream of yours."

The shepherd described the stranger in the white and green robe and how he'd foreseen his fortune on London Bridge, sold his sheep and travelled here from Wales.

The merchant roared with laughter. "Pay no attention to dreams, son, they are for fools, children, old women and priests – get a proper job and get on with your life. I had a dream last night, but I'd soon as cut my own throat as take any notice of it. I was on a high Welsh hillside in an old ruined church made of stone with no roof and an enormous oak tree. There I see buried deep under the soil between the roots of that vast oak a chest of treasure hidden in haste a long time ago by a one-eyed pirate. It's just a dream, a childish fantasy, that's all, nothing more."

But the young shepherd had vanished, heading back north and west to the hills towards the sweet-smelling pastures of the uplands he had left behind many weeks ago.

A destiny not far from home

As soon as the shepherd arrived back in the hills he started digging. He never did study but he did something else instead. He used his fortune, the pirate's treasure, profitably and in time became a wealthy merchant, the richest in those parts. With his profits he built schools, attracted the best teachers, offered scholarships for the poor and it wasn't long before his native land had as rich and diverse a culture as any other place in the kingdom.

Today you can find his statue at the centre of the town where he built his first seat of learning for the poor and underprivileged. On the pedestal are written the words: 'Follow your dream and seek it out, your fortune may be closer than you think. Notice all that is around you for it is all there to serve you. Do not miss an acorn, however small, for the acorn is father to the oak.'

"What we think determines what happens to us, so if we want to change our lives, we need to stretch our minds."

Wayne Dyer

Can you see how powerful your mind can be? You might hear a throwaway comment from someone or spot something in a lesson at school, see something at work or during a TV show that ignites a spark of imagination. Even in dreams your mind finds ways to show you ideas, solutions and innovations.

Have you heard of the phrase 'keep an open mind'? Well, exactly that, you never know where it might lead.

Chapter 20

What can you learn from our great leaders?

When you think about the word leadership, what images come to mind?

Do you see a world leader, a businessperson or a politician or famous actor standing behind a podium on a stage addressing a huge crowd of people?

What is leadership?

This is a question I've asked many people of all ages, in various careers, with different educations and backgrounds. And, as you would expect, I've had many replies and differences in opinion but everyone agrees that it's about stepping up and stepping forward in some way to show other people around you the way forward.

A characteristic that most leaders possess is a creative, determined or resilient mind. Many leaders focus on the spark of an idea that originated in their imagination and ran with it, taking the world with them!

"Leadership is the capacity to translate vision into reality."

Warren Bennis

What does a leader do?

Have you ever heard the phrase 'do as I say, not as I do'?

Leadership is about being able to communicate a message to others in a way that's effective. A way that encourages people to stand together and move forward in strength. 'Do as I say, not as I do' is a conflicting statement that suggests the person speaking those words is not doing something right. So, why should they be a leader?

Leadership can be making tough decisions and getting stuff done but there's so much more to it. The world needs young people like you and those young at heart to step up and step forward for what you believe in.

What makes a leader?

This is a great question because it's not like you wake up one morning and hey presto, you're a leader. You don't instantly become a leader because someone who holds power such as the Queen honours you to have a leadership role.

Leaders come from all walks of life. They can be of any age, race, gender and have a multitude of characteristics.

Sometimes people find themselves in a leadership role as if by accident. Maybe at school as head girl or boy or through a job promotion. For some, leadership skills come naturally and friends, classmates or colleagues respect your decisions and 'follow' you from the start, but for others, the skills or knowledge is learned.

No matter who or what the situation, leadership is an important role because it's one that puts you in the limelight, requires a level of responsibility and lays the foundation for positive change.

What does it take to become a leader?

Do you need confidence to be a leader? To be respected, inspirational, passionate or a great communicator and with a mission or a message to share?

Think back to the first vision you had of a leader at the beginning of this chapter. What attributes did the person in your vision have? What attributes would someone need in order for you to follow their lead?

If you are unsure about this, think about who you follow at the moment. Do you follow every social media post published by a film star, pop star, theatre actor, sports person or environmental activist? What newsletters, YouTube channels or podcasts do you subscribe to?

Do you follow individuals who are mentors, teachers, a family member, friends or classmates? There are probably many people who you admire and follow for different reasons. Work out what they are because this will give you an insight into what you value as an individual.

"A leader is a dealer in hope."

Napoleon Bonaparte

Who are our great leaders?

There are many types of leader and leadership styles. I want to share the names of four leaders who achieved big time when they held a leadership role.

I want you to think of what you know about these people and how you perceive them as a person and their achievements. If you are not familiar with these famous figures from the past (and present), spend five minutes researching each of them to improve your knowledge – you never know when they may come up in a question at the next pub quiz.

- Winston Churchill – UK Prime Minister who led the country through World War Two

- Mahatma Gandhi – led India to independence

- Martin Luther King Jr. – American Christian minister who led the civil rights movement from 1955

- Bill Gates – American businessman, co-founder of Microsoft Corporation and now philanthropist

On a scale of one to ten (ten being the highest) how would you rate these leaders in terms of:

- Positivity

- Effectiveness

- Empowerment

- Discipline

- Trust

- Confidence
- Ambassador for their cause
- Relationship-building
- Achievement
- Communication

Winston Churchill liked to lead from the front and empowered his followers to stand up for what they believed in. He had high standards, chose his team wisely and stood by his morals not to surrender when the nation was at war.

Gandhi was an ambassador and a leader who was good at making other people feel valued. He liked the personal touch and built solid relationships with those around him and led by example in a non-violent, very peaceful protest.

Martin Luther King Jr. used his intelligence (rather than his heart), peaceful philosophy and strong communication to lead a non-violent movement in a non-violent way.

Bill Gates is a strong innovative leader who encouraged creativity, innovation and recognised individual and team achievements.

What great leaders can you think of past and present? Can you identify anybody who you think will rise above the rest to become a great leader?

"A leader is one who knows the way, goes the way and shows the way."

John Maxwell

Following influential (for the right reasons) leaders will help you to make better decisions, keep your mind curious and to grow and learn from their wisdom. Acknowledging the traits that you like and dislike in the people that you meet every day will help you to replicate the positive traits in your own character.

Chapter 21

How to develop inspirational leadership energy

The last chapter looked at the achievements of some of the world's greatest leaders, all of which were positive in outcome.

Yet not all leaders are good or positive or even appointed.

Sometimes leaders appoint themselves because they have their own agenda, which is often not in the best interests of the people around them. These people are referred to as dictators.

> "Become the kind of leader that people would follow voluntarily, even if you had no title or position."
>
> **Brian Tracy**

When does a leader become a dictator?

A dictator is someone who has complete power but has usually taken that control by force.

Let's simplify this. A dictator can become so because they feel they have lost control or feel threatened in some way. If they can't gain trust or support from their assumed followers, they will control them by telling them what to do.

Think about this in your own life. Do you ever try to control your brother, sister or friends in some way if they don't do what you want them to? Maybe you feel that your parents try to control you by demanding that you tidy your room, do your homework or forbid you access to something.

Think about a classroom situation or at work. If a leader (teacher or manager) loses the respect of their team or students, they might move towards demanding respect rather than inspiring and earning respect. When rewards and motivation stop working for a leader, they may try to get the results they seek in a different way, in extreme cases by inducing fear or by bullying.

A leader might start out positively, uniting people under a common cause, but this can change quickly if they come up against resistance or get a thirst for their newfound power.

Are you a good leader?

Do you believe you are a leader? Was there a resounding 'no way' in your head in answer to that question or maybe a 'not yet' or 'yes I am'? How you answer depends on your beliefs around leadership as discussed earlier.

Just as you considered who you followed, who your role models were... who sees you as a role model? What followers do you have?

Are you the organiser of family video calls, online quizzes with friends or regular catch-ups? Are you perhaps already leading but don't know it?

"Before you are a leader, success is all about growing yourself. When you become a leader, success is all about growing others."

Jack Welch

Energy leadership

I believe that we all have it within us to become a leader. Energy leadership is concerned with how you show up in the world and to those around you. There are three types of energy leaders:

- Flatline energy leader
- Negative energy leader
- Positive energy leader

The flatline energy leader is the person who has switched off their emotions and pulled the plug on their energy so that they don't feel bad. It's as though they have flatlined emotionally.

There comes a challenge with this because when you have put a lid on your emotions to stop feeling bad, you can't feel good either; you become emotionally numb, quiet and blend into the background. This state is not really living is it? It's simply surviving or existing and that's not how life is meant to be.

People with flatline energy find it hard to influence anything or anybody – even themselves because they have no drive and nothing is exciting to them. A leader with flatline energy will struggle to motivate staff or pupils, friends and classmates because they have no vibrancy that others can get behind to support.

Negative energy leaders are more obvious and you have probably met many. They moan and groan, huff, puff and tut about everything and you will hear them before they enter a room. They will often act like life owes them a living and they will use controlling techniques on those who follow them.

If you speak to a negative energy leader, even for five minutes, they are likely to leave you feeling emotionally drained. Have you heard of the phrase 'mood hoovers'? Well, that's what a person with negative energy is like, they suck the positive energy right out of you like a vacuum cleaner sucks dust out of carpet.

A positive energy leader on the other hand has a presence and you can literally feel their energy. They have an amazing ability to connect and after spending a few minutes in their company they leave you feeling positive, uplifted, inspired and energised.

So which kind of energy leader are you?

Choose your energy wisely

It's important to be consciously aware of these traits and choose wisely what type of energy you ooze because you will affect and infect the people around you. It's equally as important to choose who you spend your time with. Hanging around flatliners and mood hoovers will not serve you well. In fact, these people can drag you down very quickly until you become a miniscule part of your former positive self.

Choose to spend time with positive energy people and better still, why not become the leader yourself? Before you shrug the possibility off, you do have it in you because this book has taken you through many techniques that help you to develop a positive mindset that leads to personal leadership.

What is personal leadership?

Personal leadership is about taking control and being the leader of your own life.

For every new day that breaks, are you the leader in your own life? You are responsible for how you show up in the world in what you think, what you do and what you say.

Leading by your own standards and values and only investing time and energy into doing things that are good for you is hugely rewarding and will increase your positive energy levels. Share exciting and innovative ideas with friends and family and be that positive role model.

Blaming everything and everybody for what's going wrong in the world around you and within you is actually a manifestation of you giving away control and losing your life's energy. And that's not healthy for anyone.

Take control of your life, both in your thoughts and in your emotions, to positively affect your energy and positively infect your actions. Choose to believe that life happens for you. Everything that happens is an opportunity to learn and grow and lead your own life.

If you do have a tendency to moan and groan, stop it now. What you are actually doing is choosing to delete amazing things from your awareness by not spotting opportunities to learn and grow. Even when times in the outside world are challenging or you feel a little lost inside, draw strength deep from within and think about your personal standards and values.

"A great person attracts great people and knows how to hold them together."

Johann Wolfgang Von Goethe

What do you stand for?

What do you believe in or feel strongly about right now that you can speak up for and support? Can you use these standards and values to become a role model or mentor to others? Find your 'magnificent me' and lead by example. Create a vision for the future and share your goals in a way that inspires your friends, your brothers, sisters and parents, and your teachers and work colleagues.

You could be doing them a huge favour by gifting your positive energy to them. You have the chance to lead in so many ways, and when you are being your best self you can bring out the best in others, the best in the situation you're in and the best possible outcome for your future.

Choose to start every day with positive energy and use it to lead the way for yourself and others.

Chapter 22

Influencing behaviours for the better

Now you've had a chance to think about leadership and how great leaders radiate positive energy, let's combine this with what you know about behaviour.

Remember the 60,000 thoughts you have every single day? And how, in order to influence your own behaviour, you need to understand what drives you?

Understanding the emotions generated and subsequent behaviours of these 60,000 thoughts gives you more emotional intelligence and enables you to make confident judgment calls to stay in control of your life and live in flow.

> "Emotions can get in the way or get you on the way."
>
> **Mavis Mazhura**

Change can intensify behaviours – good or bad

Stressful times, such as a pandemic or life-changing experience in the form of a house move, change in school, marriage or even a breakup magnifies people's behaviour and as a result they meet their needs in different ways – I briefly touched on this in chapter 18.

The caring people become more caring, the selfish become more selfish, the angry become angrier, the worriers worry more and those with anxiety have panic attacks.

It's logical when you think about it because if life conditions change massively and rapidly, your thinking capabilities can't always expand fast enough to deal with what's going on.

Under pressure you evolve or crumble

By using the resources around and within you positively you will effectively evolve to meeting your needs or the needs of the situation with positive behaviours.

When you devolve (or crumble under the pressure) the resources inside are forgotten and you can go into fear and panic mode and use anxiety and anger as a coping mechanism to meet your needs, which often results in poor behaviours.

What do you see around you?

Take a moment to think about what you see in the people around you. People you know and people who you don't know. How is their behaviour?

Behaviour is the outward result of an unmet need and it's important not to judge people too harshly because the moment you do, you lose the ability to appreciate them for who they really are.

People are not their behaviours because the person can change their behaviour and that depends on the driving force. Once again, it's a circular process.

"It isn't stress that makes us fall, it's how we respond to stressful events."

Wayde Goodall

The six human needs

In *The Spark to Your Success — Helping Teens Build Resilience*, I introduced the concept of the six human needs that equate to living a balanced life. This chapter will recap the needs to build on the necessity for meeting them in a positive way.

Certainty

Everyone has a need for certainty. For you, this could be security, safety, peace of mind or a feeling of being in control of your own destination.

Now, once in a lifetime (probably) an unprecedented event might take place and, all of a sudden, you are told what to do and a new set of rules are put in place. Without warning, certainty is replaced with uncertainty and meeting that need may become negative through anger (often through fear), developing symptoms of obsessive compulsive disorder (repeating things over and over again or being over the top), feeling anxious or panic buying.

To counteract this uncertainty, structure will help. By creating structure in your day for yourself and to support people around you, you'll be better prepared and organised for what lies ahead.

Variety

The need for variety is fulfilled by learning new skills, visiting new places, trying new activities and meeting new people. You can do this in person or virtually and whilst there are plenty of choices – cooking, crafting, exercising, gaming, learning, dating – the online world isn't quite a replacement for the physical world, which leads us nicely to the human need of love and connection.

Love and connection

Are you meeting your need for love and connection by gossiping, scaremongering, or even attention seeking by being overly 'out there' or getting stressed and anxious?

Negatively meeting the need for love and connection will see 'naysayers' huddling together and moaning about the world, sympathising with each other to gain connection. It can be seen on social media too with the type of posts that crave a sympathy response. Are you an online drama king or queen?

Instead, meet your connection and love needs positively by connecting through humour, encouragement and optimism – it's far healthier. Engaging online on Instagram, Tik Tok or House Party is a great way to connect 24/7 in between meeting in person.

Can you help elderly relatives or those more disengaged from technology to reconnect with loved ones? Or what about volunteering in your local community to let people know that someone cares? It's a great act of kindness and it even tops up your own needs!

Significance

Meeting your need for significance is when you do something or receive something (such as a compliment) that makes you feel special and unique. Whilst this might sound like a good thing, many people feel significant by criticising others or attempting to take control in an undermining or disrespectful way. Think about the dictator.

The best way to meet your need for significance is to step up and take responsibility for yourself. Doing positive things through service, teaching or caring can make you a great role model to your friends, family and community.

Use your gifts to create new skills, systems and mindsets, and find a voice to spread positivity. Significance can lead to a real sense of freedom.

Learning and growth

There are so many ways to meet your need for learning and growth. Remember, what you focus on is what you get, so be different, more skilled, knowledgeable, interesting and resourceful.

What are the things available to you to learn online? The opportunities are vast and I encourage you to immerse yourself in new activities and topics that intrigue you. Embrace everything that will allow you to feel enriched and grow as a person.

They say that knowledge is power and once you realise how many new opportunities open up as you learn, you'll never want to stop!

Contribution

The final essential human need of contribution is your way of giving back.

Instead of wallowing in self-pity (for whatever reason), think about connection and kindness again. How can you serve your community, family, your parents or siblings, especially if they work hard and sacrifice things in their job or for you?

What can you do at home to contribute to making their lives a little bit easier and show that you appreciate them by easing their pressure? Can you wash the car, pull out weeds from the garden, do the ironing or offer to fetch the groceries?

Perhaps you could volunteer for a conservation campaign, check in on an elderly relative or put a card through a neighbour's door to say 'hi, I hope you're well, please reach out if you need anything'.

Find ways to meet your needs positively

Help yourself and those around you. You cannot control people's behaviours but you can stand back and observe ways to influence their behaviour for the better – and your own.

The optimism created by acting in this way is phenomenal and before you know it, you'll be on positivity auto pilot!

Chapter 23

How do you make sure you stay in control?

Throughout this book you've learned about how to create and maintain a positive mindset by keeping out the negative influences and staying in control of your own thoughts, emotions and behaviours. But what really is control?

What happens when you have control? When you feel controlled? Or when you lose control? And what happens when you take back your control?

The goal of this chapter is to act as a word of warning about the positive and negative ways to gain control and to offer a summary of the positive actions to take.

"No one has power over you unless you give it to them, you are in control of your life and your choices decide your own fate."

Anonymous

What is control?

The dictionary definition of control is:

- To order, limit or rule something, or someone's actions or behaviours. It's the act of controlling something or someone, or the power to do that

- A rule or law that sets a limit on something

- To decide or strongly influence the particular way in which something will happen or someone will behave

The definitions make perfect sense but how does it emotionally feel to be controlled or to control? In the last chapter you read that the six human needs maintain the control of balance and that control is one of your driving forces.

Feeling in control of the things that happen inside you and around you gives a sense of certainty, a feeling of safety, security, calmness, peace of mind and knowing what to expect.

When you feel like you've lost control it's a completely different feeling that can quickly turn into worry, anxiety, confusion and panic. You will feel vulnerable, threatened and afraid, and the more you focus on those feelings, the more they grow – remember, what you think, you feel and do.

"Control your thoughts and everything will be under your control."

Debasish Mridha

Taking back control with anger

If someone takes away your control, you might feel undervalued and not respected and these feelings might turn to anger. This rage tries to take back control by causing fear, dishing out threats or, in the extreme, sees you resorting to violence. Whilst this isn't the best way to take back your control, it can turn into a habit if people give in to the person displaying rage. Condoning anger as a behaviour by giving in to it actually confirms to the person that this is how you get what you want.

Imagine how this behaviour could escalate from something as seemingly trivial as a child throwing a tantrum at teatime to bringing that anger into the classroom, to the workplace or into a relationship.

Taking back control by being over-controlling

Instead of being an inspirational leader, an over-controlling person may become a dictator by commanding others as to what they must do. Over-controlling can also include the use of passive aggressive behaviours such as deliberately being late or not doing something or playing the victim. Even sulking, bullying and stubbornness is a form of over-controlling behaviour.

Controlling by using manipulative behaviour

Manipulative behaviour is a way to get people to do what you want by causing them to feel afraid of humiliation or guilt as a consequence if they don't.

As an example, if you were to say to your parents: 'If you don't let me go to the party everyone will pick on me. It will be your fault and I'll have no friends because I was the only one from my class who didn't go. Everyone's parents have said yes except you.'

Manipulative people lie, blame others and live in denial to get their own way. They will swear something did or did not happen and behave in a way that you feel sorry for them. They may even manipulate you by pretending to be on your side and go as far as to undermine your confidence, self-belief and make you feel inadequate or useless to get their way.

Controlling by micromanagement

Micromanaging things is a form of over-controlling where everything is micromanaged right down to the finest detail.

You might think that people cannot be trusted to do a task correctly therefore you oversee every minute detail of the task and question every single step: 'Have you done this yet? Did you do it right? Did you do this, this and this? Where did you put that? Why did you do that?'

When micromanaging becomes a habit, you might not trust anyone to do anything because you think they'll mess it up and will therefore do everything yourself. Again, see the circular outcome of this where you will become tired, stressed and angry at others because you receive no help… but you brought it upon yourself by micromanaging.

Controlling your environment

Controlling your environment could mean being organised, neat and tidy but it becomes a negative controlling behaviour when obsession sets in. When there's a precise place for everything or a procedure on how to do something right down to the smallest detail it can even lead to Obsessive Compulsive Disorder (OCD), such as handwashing, checking doors are locked, windows are closed and flicking the light switches over and over and over before leaving the house.

Eating disorders can develop in this way too because people know they can control what goes into their mouth.

What happens when you feel controlled?

Everything you've read so far is concerned with feeling out of control, so what happens when you feel controlled by someone or something?

Do any of the previous circumstances feel familiar to you? Think carefully about this next question: are you the one in control or being controlled?

Feeling controlled by a situation or person causes feelings of fear, resentment, helplessness and powerlessness. You may feel used, abused, manipulated and disrespected and you may start to ask questions because you are confused and unsure.

- Why me?
- Why is this happening to me?
- What can I do?

People who are controlled in some way often feel that there is no way out of a bad situation and may even start to believe that they deserve the treatment they are receiving.

If you can relate to any of this and feel that a situation or someone's behaviour towards you (or your behaviour to someone else) is bad, hard, unfair or oppressive and so on, then your unconscious mind is trying to tell you to stop. To do something differently. To claim back your power, reclaim your destiny and that has to start with you.

"When you react, you let others control you. When you respond, you are in control."

Bohdi Sanders

Stay in control responsibly

The best way to make sure you stay in control is to take back responsibility for your thoughts, your feelings, your actions and your interactions with the people around you. Recognise that this is your world too.

Start by changing what goes on inside your own head and make it positive. Every. Single. Day. Here are some ideal ways to start:

- Catch the little things that make you smile and laugh and consequently feel happier

- Be kind to others, just because you can

- Be more organised, on time and do things first time when you're asked. Even better, surprise other people by doing things in advance rather than last minute

- Look for the good in every situation. Believe that everything happens for a positive reason, even if it doesn't feel that way at the time, so find fun in seeking out the positive

- Ask how you can help others rather than waiting to be told and then moan that you're being told what to do

- Make your own decisions rather than waiting for others to make them for you

- Decide what you stand for and think for yourself

- Do your own research, plan ahead and build resilience

The above bullet points are simple ways to ensure that you feel a sense of certainty, peace of mind and calmness. You will feel energised and balanced because you have met your needs positively.

"Life does not control you.
What you believe about it does."

Alan Cohen

You can't control the outside world, but you can control your inside world, your mindset and how you interpret meaning.

Chapter 24

Goal setting – plot your future

I've touched on the importance of goal setting in previous chapters but now I want you to put this into practice by outlining your future goals.

Here's a handy chart for you to download:

www.backontrackteens.com/wp-content/uploads/2021/03/Wheel-of-Life-BOTT.pdf

What do you want to achieve?

Goal setting can be a huge task. In order to be successful in achieving your goals you need to give them some careful thought and set realistic expectations. When a goal isn't met, it's easy to beat yourself up, which isn't good for anybody – yourself or the people around you.

Not achieving a goal can be due to a number of reasons. Setting an unrealistic goal in the first place is the biggie, but so is losing focus or not re-evaluating when unexpected obstacles get in the way.

So, what's the answer?

Commit to good habits

When you make a commitment to start something new and work towards a goal, it doesn't have to be a giant step. In fact, taking small baby steps makes it easier to build new habits and stick to them. If new habits are small yet consistent you will be amazed at how quickly they add up to a bigger journey with visible progress.

Start small

When I was younger, I built an exercise 'hour of power' habit every morning. I would get up, complete my exercise routine and post what I had done online as a way of keeping myself accountable and (hopefully) inspiring others to do the same.

You might think that an hour every morning before you get ready for school or work sounds impossible because there isn't enough time. You might think that because of the commitments you already have you won't be able to commit to it consistently. And that's OK.

The worst thing to do is attempt a goal that is too big or unachievable because you are setting yourself up to fail from the word go and you'll only feel fed up with yourself for it.

If this is the case, instead of jumping straight into an hour of intensive cardio, start where you feel comfortable, such as a 20-minute body toning session for a set number of days. Be realistic, celebrate your successes and build from there.

"All who have accomplished great things have had a great aim, have fixed their gaze on a goal which was high, one which sometimes seemed impossible."

Orison Swett Marden

Ready, steady, set your goals

Print off a copy of the goal-setting chart from the start of the chapter or open it on your laptop. You will need some time to complete this exercise so switch off any interruptions, nip to the loo or grab a bite to eat and a drink (remember how easy it is to get distracted?).

When you are completely relaxed, think about what you want from your future.

- What would you like to do better?
- If something would make you happier, what would that be?
- What do you need in order to start your ideal career?
- Who do you want to be around?

Consider the eight segments in the wheel of life. What goals can you set (remember to start small) in order to improve how you feel about these areas of your life.

- Family
- Work or education
- Friends
- Wellbeing
- Relationships
- Adventure

- Money
- Home

If you're struggling to think of any goals, could you develop your writing or reading skills, take regular exercise, meditate, learn a language, play an instrument or get better at studying for your exams?

There are so many possibilities and variations to choose from. Imagine what you really want in life and create a powerful vision in your mind. Remember the shepherd who went to London Bridge after his dream? What can you commit to doing now that will help your journey? Start today.

Form new and exciting habits to improve areas of your health, education, positive emotions and actions with yourself and others, and be more adventurous.

"If you want to be happy, set a goal that commands your thoughts, liberates your energy and inspires your hopes."

Andrew Carnegie

Create a rule of 20

To help you develop small and achievable goals, think about them as something you complete in a 20-minute session each day to build a habit.

It doesn't even have to be time that you commit to. It could be 20 things, such as 20 press-ups, sit-ups or squats for 20 days as a health goal. What about starting a journal and writing down 20 things that you are grateful for each day?

Every morning start the day with a positive mindset by logging what you are looking to achieve on that day. Then at night list everything positive that has happened during the day, including things that you love about yourself or the people around you.

Your goal might be to meet 20 new people, read 20 books or visit 20 new places over the course of the next year.

Commitment helps you to feel proud. It's the start of a journey. A journey about who you want to be and over time, each habit will become automatic, so you can keep committing to more small habits that will lead to a bigger dream.

"By recording your dreams and goals on paper, you set in motion the process of becoming the person you most want to be. Put your future in good hands — your own."

Mark Victor Hansen

Pick something small and do it consistently to create a new habit and have the discipline to see it through to the end.

Chapter 25
The circle of life

This entire book has introduced you to creativity, innovation, open-minded thinking and a positive mindset. You have learned about how your thoughts, emotions and actions can be affected in different ways by what you let into your mind from the outside world such as the media, other people and resources. It's also important to reflect and acknowledge decisions made and actions taken with the benefit of hindsight.

As this book draws to an end, your tomorrow will start with a completely new, focused and positive outlook on life.

Show yourself in a positive light

Set yourself up as you mean to progress in life as future parents, leaders, lovers and businesspeople and bring self-discipline into your life today.

Start each day with your why, your vision. Imagine what you want to see and hear. What will it feel like to touch? What will it make you feel like inside? Set goals and visualise them as much as possible so that they become a reality more quickly.

Once you have goals, find people that will hold you accountable, ensure your standards and values are met and who love you enough to be consistent and have a firm word if necessary.

Obstacles will always challenge your thinking, but if you stay true to who you are and block out the negativity of other people (individuals, organisations and the media), you will rise above it to find new ways to succeed.

Maintain balance in life and know that it starts from within. What you do begins from deep within your mind and it's a circular process. Think bad and bad things will happen. Think positive and positive things will happen.

All that you need is right with you, right now – your positive mindset.

Chapter 26

Wake up happy tomorrow and spring into action

I hope you've been on a journey reading this book. I hope, too, that you have felt some inner realisations by reflecting on the past and about what you want from the future. Please remember that this book (and the others in the *Spark to Your Success* series) are only the start. The exercises have been designed to make you think on a deeper level, to question your thoughts and actions and those of others.

What you take from the resources and newfound knowledge is your choice. It's OK to make mistakes, but you choose how to react to the experiences you have. This book and my teachings are here to support you with the growth of your mindset and to balance the positives and negatives in life.

Now let's make sure you wake up happy tomorrow and spring into action.

Bursting with vitality

It should be exciting to start a new day. Granted it's easier to get up and get on during the spring and summer months because of the longer and lighter days, but every day throughout the year holds an abundance of opportunity, so let's get bouncy!

'Bounce out of bed in the morning, really?' I hear you say! 'It takes effort to roll out of bed after whacking the alarm for the sixth time.'

If this is you, keep reading to explore how to wake up happy and *want* to leap into your day!

What wakes you up?

Let me start by asking you a question: "How do you know when it is time to wake up?"

Is it the sound of the birds singing outside your window, the gentle rays of sunshine peeping into your room or (more likely) is it the harsh sound of an alarm, the shouting of a parent or the jumping on your bed by a younger sibling or a slobbering pet?

The thought of an alarm buzzing harshly or someone screaming at me to get out of bed isn't exactly encouraging nor is it a great way to start your day, so let's think about how to reset the morning wake-up routine for a better awakening.

I've written blogs about the importance of getting enough sleep, eating healthily and trying relaxing, stress-reducing activities such as meditation and practising mindfulness.

Check out some of the past blogs to help your body clock work more efficiently here: www.backontrackteens.com/blog/

For now, let's take a look at how to wake up happy.

How to wake up happy

The sound that wakes you up is important because it can set the scene for the entire day.

Invest in a daylight alarm clock, which gradually makes your room lighter by simulating the natural process of a new day breaking. Gentle sounds emerge as the wake-up noise so that they are far from alarming, helping to create a positive mood.

What about waking up to something happy, bright and energetic like a cheerful song? What's your favourite happy song? One that always makes you smile and is almost hypnotic in making you sing and dance. Here's my top ten as a little inspiration:

- **Coldplay - 'Viva La Vida'**

  Get up ruling the world – what a great thought to wake up to.

- **Katrina & The Waves - 'Walking on Sunshine'**

  Such a classic tune and I dare you not to smile, move and sing along to this one!

- **The Vamps - 'Wake Up'**

  You've been deep in a coma – apt first words ☺ So wake up your sleeping heart and we will dream a dream for us that no one else can touch!

  OK, so maybe the connection isn't there with those songs, but these are surely spot on…

- **Pharrell Williams - 'Happy'**

  It might seem crazy what I'm 'bout to say… what a great way to start the day!

- **Avicii - 'Wake Me Up'**

Chapter 25

- **Bill Withers - 'Lovely Day'**

  How can you not smile to this one, it's an awesome tune to wake up to! If you are too young to remember it, Google it and give it a chance.

- **Kanye West - 'Good Morning'**

  Good morning on the day we become legendary! Fabulous lyrics to inspire your thoughts for the day ahead.

- **James Brown - 'Get Up Offa That Thing'**

  Yes! Get up offa that thing and dance until you feel better! You'll be boogieing into the bathroom in no time with this one!

- **WHAM! - 'Wake Me Up Before You Go Go'**

- **Bob Marley - 'Three Little Birds'**

I have had so much fun listening, dancing and singing loudly to these songs as I chose them for this article, and I encourage you to visit the links and add the ones you like to your own playlist of positive happy tunes. Leave out the doom and gloom!

Here is a list of the links for the tunes above:

Coldplay:
www.youtube.com/watch?v=dvgZkm1xWPE

Katrina and the Waves:
www.youtube.com/watch?v=iPUmE-tne5U

The Vamps:
www.youtube.com/e12KryuLcbs

Pharrell Williams:
www.youtube.com/watch?v=ZbZSe6N_BXs

Avicii:
www.youtube.com/watch?v=IcrbM11_BoI

Bill Withers:
www.youtube.com/watch?v=bEeaS6fuUoA

Kanye West:
www.youtube.com/watch?v=6CHs4x2uqcQ

James Brown:
www.youtube.com/watch?v=1_uNMy20qAI

WHAM!:
www.youtube.com/watch?v=pIgZ7gMze7A

Bob Marley:
www.youtube.com/watch?v=LanCLS_hIo4

Back to the waking up happy process – train your brain

First of all, wake up the right way with your happy tunes and then *train your brain* so that the first thought you think is a positive one. The thought could be inspired by your happy tune or simply by smiling as you wake and being grateful.

When you wake say thank you for a new day, thank you for a great sleep, thank you for a fresh opportunity and thank you for being who you are. Take a few moments to *intentionally* feel good before you feel or think anything else.

It might take a bit of practice, especially if you're not used to thinking in this way, but it makes a big difference.

"Limitations live only in our minds. But if we use our imaginations, our possibilities become limitless."

Jamie Paolinetti

Start your day with an intention

It helps if you fall asleep with the intention of waking up happy because your unconscious mind is amazing and will do what you direct it to do before you go to sleep.

A few years ago I trained myself to wake up with the thoughts of 'do it as well as think it'. I had my gym kit on the floor next to my bed and I trained myself to physically get into my exercise gear, go downstairs and start the day with exercise. It was awesome because I started my day with an hour of power and was pumped for the rest of day.

Recently, I have trained myself to say thank you, smile to myself and say today is a magnificent day and I am going to be magnificent in it in my own way.

This might be a stretch too far for you if you are a habitual snooze button presser, struggle to get up in the morning and finally rise at the last possible minute. Hear me out anyway…

A great way to start the day is to set your alarm earlier and instead of hitting snooze, get up and exercise, even if it's for 15 minutes. If that is beyond your mindset right now, how about getting up and after you are washed and dressed, sit and meditate for five to 15 minutes? I say after you are up and dressed because the danger is, if you sit up in bed and do it you'll fall back to sleep – and then you'll oversleep and panic when you wake up again and you're late!

If that is all too much, wake up to your happy wake-up music and keep the positive vibes flowing with an upbeat playlist till you dance your way out of the door. You'll leave feeling awesome with a smile on your face and the day will already be a success.

Spring into action every morning, keep the positivity flowing and see what an amazing difference it makes to your life. The quote below says it all for me. Thank you from the bottom of my heart for reading this book and please do connect with the Back on Track Teens community online and share your journey.

"Make each day your masterpiece."

John Wooden

Chapter 26

Connect with us:

- www.instagram.com/ignition.rocks
- www.facebook.com/IgnitionY
- teejay@backontrackteens.com

About the author

TeeJay's journey from student technician to pharmacist to neurostrategist and NLP trainer has been an amazing adventure over the last decade, and testimony to the fact that small dreams can turn into huge aspirations and the realisation of them.

"From the innocent age of four, I had a strong belief that I wasn't good enough. This negative emotion set me on a pathway in life where I never felt as though my face fitted – I was a loner, painfully shy and kept encountering obstacles in my career and social life.

"That belief stayed at my side for over three decades, tugging at my confidence and making life incredibly uncomfortable. Not once did anyone share the thought that I should *just be myself and believe in the real me, and that **I** was magnificent in my own unique skin.*

"I took a job instead of a career, was bullied at work, became a single parent at 19, endured a string of failed relationships, and found my escape by being emotionally numb to just get through each day. That is until LIFE intervened and gave me a wake-up call!"

Today TeeJay is the founder and CEO of Ignition! Coaching and Training and Back on Track Teens – two international self-development organisations that create partnerships with parents, youth coaches, communities and companies around the globe to maximise the transformation of a generation. She is a published author, international trainer, speaker and coach, and her purpose in life is to empower 10 million young people to become tomorrow's confident, successful leaders, by feeling happy in their own skin.

Notes

Notes

Notes

Notes

Notes